T0040277

PAST LIVES
UNVEILED

PAST LIVES
UNVEILED

*Discover how consciousness
moves between lives*

BARRY EATON

ROCKPOOL

Acknowledgements

To my partner Anne, who is always there for me, along with other members of my soul family, here and on the other side of the veil.

I would like to express my gratitude to Peter Smith for his support and advice, which has made this research into the past come alive in so many ways. My thanks to those people who allowed me to share their stories: Dr Norm Shealy, Walter Semkiw, Tom Smith, Sharon Prince and my oldest and dearest friend Roger Cook.

Thanks also to the team at Rockpool Publishing, Lisa, Paul, Andres and Jessica for their ongoing support in helping me open doors to the past. Finally to Lisa Macken, whose eagle-eyed editing kept me firmly on track.

A Rockpool book
PO Box 252
Summer Hill, NSW 2130
rockpoolpublishing.co
Follow us! f @ rockpoolpublishing
Tag your images with #rockpoolpublishing

First published in 2019
Copyright text © Barry Eaton, 2019

ISBN 978-1-925682-86-1

A catalogue record for this book is available from the National Library
of Australia.

Design by Jessica Le, Rockpool Publishing
Editing by Lisa Macken
Printed and bound in China

10 9 8 7 6 5 4 3 2

Contents

INTRODUCTION

I t's time for us to acknowledge that we are so much more than we know.

Throughout time we have been receiving messages from a variety of sources, although somewhere, somehow, in the Western world we have forgotten our magnificence. We have failed to remember our divine spark, our multidimensional state of being. We are simply magnificent beyond our wildest dreams, our greatest hopes and our human understanding.

When Barry Eaton told me that the intention for his next book was to go beyond the normal chronicles of past-life books into something more I was intrigued at first; then, after I'd felt into it, my heart sang and my soul started to soar.

Life-changing books can only be written by a certain type of person, and for my mind that person needs two characteristics. First, to have a purpose to serve humanity by being part of something greater than themselves and, second, to have a deep personal understanding of the subject that makes them an expert in their field. This is one of those books, and Barry is one of these people.

Barry's background as a phenomenal communicator in the media industry, a lifelong advocate of the metaphysical realms and his ability as a gifted storyteller bring to life the different angles of reincarnation evidence, anecdotes and personal experiences in a way I haven't seen before. I have absolutely no doubt he is seen from the other side as an ambassador to get the word out about who we really are, to assist in the evolution of consciousness on this planet as we know it.

For the past 13 years I've been closely associated with the Newton Institute, the last eight as global president of our organisation. With 200 highly trained afterlife practitioners in 40 countries, we have seen something like 40,000 cases take place in that period. I can tell you with full authority that people are waking up and that past lives are a path to discovering an immortal aspect of ourselves that simply transcends human understanding and sets us free.

Imagine a world where we all knew we were returning to repair relationships and situations again and again till we learn the intended lesson. What would this mean for the kindness we could show each other as soul brethren on a journey rather than competitors for scarce resources?

Imagine a world where there was no fear of death and we saw this as merely stepping into the next room. The greatest fear that permeates our society and underpins all others would then be released, and the limited understanding of our mortality would simply collapse like a house of cards. This is what we can understand as a collective, and the mindset shifts we most need to do this are echoed in the pages that follow.

I first met Barry at an afterlife conference at which I was a keynote speaker and he was an organiser, speaker and the master of ceremonies. In those three days we formed a friendship born out of deep respect and admiration for the work of each other, a shared sense of humour and, later on, a love of some very human sports like rugby and cricket.

As this book project unfolded, Barry and I chatted regularly by phone and even on his popular radio program *RadioOutThere*, which has become a community for metaphysicians, scientists and psychic intuitives from all over the world. The cases that emerged and the research undertaken by Barry drew on the work of many credible people and bodies of work, all carrying the central theme that Barry so eloquently articulates: 'We are more ... and it is time we remembered.'

So how far does this remembering go? This is a universe of unlimited proportions, much of which exists beyond time and space as we know it. If our consciousness moves between lives, where else can it go? Barry touches on this theme also as we move beyond the realms of an earthly existence. All we have to do is stop for just a moment, to remember we really only know one planet well – this one, and it is teeming with life. Can we really be arrogant enough to think that among the billions of stars and trillions of planets out there, we are all there is?

When I founded the Institute for Quantum Consciousness, we started to research other vehicles of consciousness we could experience as part of the ever-evolving lineage of our souls. So much more can be learned from those experiences, and Barry shares with us critical messages for humanity that contribute to his greater purpose through his writings over the years, and even more importantly now as we reach a point in our history when we all need to think differently.

Science has served us well in many ways, though the true nature of science is to explore new horizons, to seek and understand that which has not yet been discovered. As science steps back from this original intention when it comes to the metaphysical, there are many in the consciousness movement globally who are challenging the paradigms of the day in an effort to unearth new and amazing discoveries that change the way we see ourselves in an ever-unfolding universe of divine creation. If we truly live holographically then our own change of mindset ripples out into the universe itself, heralding a change of vibration, wisdom and knowledge.

We have the free will to do that right now. I really encourage all of you to pick up where science leaves off, to be an advocate for your own consciousness and exploration. May this book be not only your permission to do so, but a catalyst for your awakening.

As a long-term teacher, practitioner and leader in this field, I offer you some practical guidance. Undertake these journeys with someone of pure intent and advanced skill. Past-life work and beyond can be complicated, and sometimes deeply therapeutic work is required in altered states. Please check the credentials of the person you ask to take you on such journeys. Feel beyond what you read on a website and move into your heart; your soul will guide you to the right person.

Having had the chance to work with Barry on this project has been such an honour for me. To witness first hand the loving energy, sharp mind and heart-based efforts of the next part of

Barry's purpose to serve humanity has been an absolute privilege.

Science continues to search for the 'theory of everything', believing that we can have just one theory that underpins how the universe works. I don't feel we will ever discover with our limited human intellect how everything 'works'. However, if we move beyond the human intellect and the hard-wired physiology that we are, if we expand metaphysically into realms yet to be explored, we may just find this energy that holds everything together ... may just be the energy of love.

Enjoy your journey through the pages ahead.

Peter Smith

President, Newton Institute for Life between Lives Hypnotherapy

Founder, Institute for Quantum Consciousness

Chapter 1

THE CONCEPT OF
REINCARNATION AND PAST LIVES

When we are born into each lifetime on Earth a subconscious veil is lowered that separates us from the world of spirit, where our soul resides in between lifetimes. This separation allows us to fully experience life in a new body without memories of previous incarnations crowding our conscious mind, potentially obstructing our growth and development. Life is challenging enough without the past flooding into the mind, creating unnecessary confusion and other emotional or physical distractions. However, choosing to uncover our past lives at the right time can be extremely helpful and healing.

My purpose is to lift the veil, to investigate and explore this hidden aspect of our lives.

My fascination with past lives has led me to discover several of my previous incarnations, with the view to understanding more about who I am and what my purpose is in this life. The results have been at times most unexpected, but on the whole are best described as being life changing.

Most of us skim through life preoccupied with the material

objectives associated with career, family, friends, real estate and leisure activities. More and more our lives are being carefully programmed and controlled by the advertising and marketing industries, with a huge range of products and temptations being thrust at us on a daily basis. In the frenetic times we associate with life in the 21st century in the Western world there seems to be little time left to explore our inner world, let alone contemplate our spiritual purpose. Fortunately, more and more people are taking time out to contemplate such questions as: what is the purpose of life, where do we come from, are we alone in the universe, and what does the future hold in these challenging times?

Logically, each one of us is the product of what has gone on in our life prior to this current moment. The events of our lives — from early environment, through our formative years to the present stage of our existence — have shaped each of us into the unique individual we are today. The question is, however: are we confining this state of being to only one life, the one we are living now?

Having written two books about life after death, *Afterlife* and *No Goodbyes*, my research into the world of spirit indicates that each incarnation contains many destiny points along the way, but it is up to our free will to choose what action we decide to take. It is like the script of a movie, which contains what are known as 'plot points', and the decisions made by the characters direct the next sequence of the story.

Unfortunately, in real life most of us are too preoccupied to even notice some of these destiny points and life just keeps drifting on. That is, unless that event is so serious we are virtually forced to emerge from our self-created bubble to face the situation at hand and make a decision to act in some way. This may also entail putting our life on hold as we search for answers to a confronting problem, and take actions and make decisions that may have a big impact on us as individuals and those around us at the time.

Exploring our past lives often explains why we have these destiny points in each lifetime, and can help with making the best decisions to move on successfully and leave the past behind. Investigating my own past has provided me with many answers about my current life and its primary purpose. It is my intention with this book to open hidden doors to the past so we can all benefit from the many past-life experiences of the wide-ranging group of people I have been fortunate to meet as part of my research.

There are many ways to explore past lives, but I have found that hypnotherapy tops the list for accuracy and credibility. I have worked with hypnotherapy in several different past-life regressions over the last 35 years or so and have had many memorable experiences, some of which are recalled in this book. I have been taken to experience past lives in ancient Egypt as a priest, Roman-occupied Cairo as a Roman soldier, a healer/wise woman in an eighth-century Central American jungle village, Damascus in the Middle Ages, two lives in mediaeval France (one as a nun), and my immediate past life produced vivid memories as a young British soldier killed in France in the 1916 offensive on the Somme.

In none of these lives was I anybody famous or even notable. They were all average people, and over the centuries I have lived as both man and woman. While researching my books I did manage to ascertain that I also had many lives as a soldier or warrior, but by the time of my death in the Great War I had apparently cleared all the karma associated with my military violence over many lifetimes and could put it all behind me. Despite a lifelong fascination with the events of First World War I haven't had any involvement with soldiering in this life, apart from four years spent in the army cadets at school. In fact, I did contemplate naval officer training when I left school but was disqualified for medical reasons. So it appears that I really have learned and moved on from my military past.

When I started my high school studies many years ago, my ancient history teacher told us that studying the past always fascinated him because the more he learned the more he came to realise that history moves in cycles. This life has taught me that we keep repeating the same mistakes, evidenced by the rise and fall of governments, countries, empires and civilisations. Seemingly always at war somewhere in the world, we never appear to learn from the past.

The ancient Roman statesman and philosopher Marcus Tullius Cicero summed it up well in one of his famous quotes: 'The budget should be balanced, the treasury refilled, public debt reduced, the arrogance of officialdom tempered and controlled, and the assistance to foreign lands curtailed, lest Rome become bankrupt.'

My teacher's thought has stayed with me ever since, and often comes to mind as I observe current events that so often echo the past. Perhaps that is one reason why the whole subject of past lives and reincarnation has always intrigued me.

I embraced the principle of reincarnation from a very young

age, knowing intuitively that our current lifetime is just one of many over a vast span of 'time'. I have always wondered why, if there is only one shot at life, the playing field is so uneven. Why are some people born in abject poverty, struggling to merely survive, while others have everything served up on a golden platter? My heartfelt belief, supported by extensive research in the last thirty years or so, is that we come to Earth on many journeys of self-growth and spiritual development and this can only happen when we go through a vast array of life experiences. Each incarnation offers us another lifetime to grow spiritually via these experiences, and what we do with the many opportunities that arise is up to each one of us.

Broadly speaking, my research confirms for me that we reincarnate on Earth with a wide variety of people, experiencing many different cultures and locations. However, there is a close band of souls we return with during many of these lives, especially those very close to us as family, friends, colleagues and even adversaries. This includes members of our immediate and extended soul families, and often our most intense relationships are with those with whom we have shared many past lives. I will go into the area of soul relationships in detail in a separate chapter.

Most people can remember meeting someone for the first time and feeling a great sense of familiarity, almost as if they know them already. It would be interesting to know how many long-term relationships begin under these circumstances; it could also be a key reason for 'love at first sight'. This sense of deeply buried memories can take many forms, not only involving personal relationships. You may visit a city that you've never been to before yet somehow you recognise streets and buildings. You start playing a new sport and amaze everyone, including yourself, at your natural abilities and intuitive knowing of the rules.

We are often given clues to previous lives when experiencing a sense of *déjà vu*; a place, a situation or even a person could resonate so strongly with us that bells ring in our intuition. Many people remember visiting a city, town or even a street that is somehow very familiar, even though they have never been there in this lifetime. A certain period, or even an event in history, may also create unusually high interest for no apparent reason.

When I unexpectedly decided to do a diploma course in astrology in 1991, in my first lecture I would have been stretched to name all twelve zodiac signs. I was going through a personal transformation at the time following a marriage breakdown, and was drawn to this course through responding to some inner message. All those planets and strange symbols were very confusing at first, but I resisted the temptation to bail out and hung in there. After a few weeks it was as if some kind of fog had lifted from my brain, and everything fell into place. From that moment on I had little or no difficulty understanding the complexities of this ancient science.

To pass the course we all had to get a 100 per cent score in the final test, a feat I had never even come close to in any previous studies. My classmates all had some previous knowledge or experience with astrology, so I was behind the eight ball, so to speak. Not only did I score a perfect result; I got my diploma only nine months after starting this course as a complete novice. My teacher, Garry Wiseman, told me it was the fastest he had ever seen a student graduate from one of his courses.

While I have not yet been able to prove this was a result of past-life learning, I do feel there is in some way a connection with my past and that renewing my love of astrology is a part of my destiny in this life. Perhaps a past-life regression at a future stage will produce some evidence.

As I have come to learn in my many years on Earth, the past is alive in all of us.

'The intuitive mind is a sacred gift and the rational mind is a faithful servant. We have created a society that honors the servant and has forgotten the gift.' — Albert Einstein

Chapter 2

THE RELEVANCE OF PAST LIVES

It goes without saying we are all living our lives very differently now from those of our ancestors and even the way of our parents. The pace of 21st century life is all too often frenetic and overwhelming as we cope with rapid change and the ever-evolving technology that sees information bombarding us from all sides. The resulting stress from this digital overload is an inevitable part of the quickening of modern Western society. For the younger generations life is for living to the fullest – now! Who has time to worry about the future, or even concern themselves with events of the past? However, as we mature we have more time to reflect on issues such as whether or not there is an afterlife, or if indeed our current life is just one of many.

The very concept of past lives is dismissed as irrelevant by those people caught up in just getting through the daily grind, existing from one week to the next. But what if we were able to alleviate some of that pressure, to heal those physical and emotional stumbling blocks simply by understanding who we really are and what our purpose is in the grander scheme of things? Life could be even more enjoyable and certainly less stressful. We all have our special purpose in coming to this planet. Unfortunately, not many people have discovered that purpose or even bothered to look for it.

For me, the principle of reincarnation is logical. The very idea that we only get one shot at life is ridiculous. Every human being on the planet is enjoying their own unique experience, and each person's story is like a movie as it unfolds in its own individual direction. The concept of having one single lifetime just does not make sense when you think about it, especially when you look at the vastly different circumstances people find themselves in from the time of their birth. Some lives last only a matter of hours, while others live on for over a century. Where is the balance or purpose in having only one life opportunity? What would be the point of existence if birth is merely some kind of accident, the result perhaps of being allocated a number is some vast cosmic lottery? More to the point, who or what is conducting this lottery and why?

Past-life expert and former psychologist Peter Ramster writes in his book *The Search for Lives Past* (Somerset Film and Publishing Pty Ltd, 1992) that there are many benefits to be had from the acceptance of reincarnation. First, it removes the fear of death as being the end of everything. Second, it gives us purpose, 'as it is said each earthly incarnation is devised for learning'. And third, beliefs around reincarnation include karma as 'a true, just judgement during life and after death'. Past-life research has uncovered enigmas that surely can only be explained by accepting reincarnation. Under hypnosis, many people have been recorded as speaking intelligibly in a foreign language they had not learned normally in this lifetime. This is known as *xenoglossia*, which means 'foreign tongue'.

Dr Ian Stevenson, who was famous for his past-life work with children (see Chapter 9), wrote about this phenomena in his book *Xenoglossy* (University Press of Virginia, 1974). In one case he hypnotised the wife of a well-known Philadelphian doctor who started speaking Swedish. She had never been to Sweden nor learned that language. Dr Stevenson was able to consult experts who confirmed the man she connected with in the regression was speaking Swedish fluently with an authentic accent.

Dr Stevenson also recorded case studies of children bringing back phobias from previous lives, including connections with the death in that lifetime. Current birthmarks associated with the causes of previous deaths, including scars and other physical conditions, are part of his painstaking research.

The universe is too ordered to allow for the creation of a random one-life scenario. Once we accept that everything works in evolutionary cycles — planets, stars, galaxies, nature, including even the weather — it is easier to accept that we as individuals are part of that universal cycle.

We take for granted that nature works in cycles. Trees, for example, are born from a seed, grow to maturity, bloom, lose their leaves in the winter (if they're deciduous) and then bloom again. They contribute to the environment by providing oxygen, improving air quality and land (climate amelioration), conserving water, preserving soil and supporting wildlife. During the process of photosynthesis, trees take in carbon dioxide and produce some of the oxygen we breathe. When they have completed their purpose they die, but not before they have shed their seeds for further propagation. And so the cycle continues.

A child genius such as Wolfgang Amadeus Mozart is a classic example. In 1762, Wolfgang's father took him at the age of six with his older sister Nannerl, aged 11, to the court of Bavaria in Munich in what was to become the first of several European 'tours.' The siblings travelled to the courts of Paris, London, The Hague and Zurich to perform as child prodigies.

Child prodigies continue to amaze the world today; for example, Amira Willighagen, who was born in Holland in 2004 and at the age of nine auditioned for the national TV Show *Holland's Got Talent*. The judges were bemused and almost dismissive of this young girl when she told them she was going to sing an operatic aria … that is, until she started to sing and the soprano voice that emerged sounded more like that of a 29 year old. The judges were astounded, giving her a standing ovation, and could hardly believe their ears when she sweetly informed them she had taught herself to sing by looking at YouTube videos of operatic songs and had never had a singing lesson in her life.

The chief judge, Gordon Heuckeroth, summed up his feelings this way: 'They say old souls live on in people and when I hear you sing you sound just like Maria Callas. Your voice is so pure and so beautiful I find it so special for a girl of your age to be able to do this. It is incredible!'

Amira was given a golden ticket that took her straight to the finals, where she convincingly won the award. Amira is now singing professionally at a very young age and has made many international appearances in what seems to be just the beginning of an exciting career.

The question remains: is Amira the reincarnation of Maria Callas, who has returned to take her stellar career to new levels, or is she perhaps, as Gordon Heuckeroth said, just a very old soul? We may never know the answer to that question but it is worth thinking about.

Many spiritual practices and religions such as Buddhism, Hinduism and Jainism are based on the principle of reincarnation being a vital aspect of soul development. Many other religions both ancient and modern have accepted the principle of reincarnation in some form or another (see https://reincarnationafterdeath.com for more details). Our souls return to Earth over a series of lifetimes to evolve, learn, grow, transform and become more spiritually attuned through the course of each life. When we reincarnate, it is believed that we tend to cycle through our different lives with many of the same people. Often these travelling 'soul' companions are the ones we enter into relationships with; we work through our unresolved issues together so that we may heal, or help others to do so. When we struggle or keep encountering blocks that keep us from reaching our goals, there may be a specific lesson we are supposed to learn in this lifetime. Being naturally blessed with a musical talent or sporting prowess, for example, can be a special ability you worked hard to develop in a past life.

Over many lifetimes we all live as both males and females, experiencing a wide range of social and economic situations. Each lifetime brings with it specific lessons that are necessary for our spiritual evolution.

Past-life recall can give us valuable insights into our past, present and even future lives. The knowledge of how we lived before can help us overcome present obstacles, rationalise phobias, understand emotional blockages and resolve certain relationship issues. There are workshops and courses available to learn about past lives, and past-life regression therapists can guide us on our journey through time and space. We can also learn to visit our past lives through our dreams, meditation and trance work. Given the right circumstances, it is even possible to see full scenes of a former lifetime flash before us in our mind's eye as if we were watching a movie.

Numerous books have been written about this subject and case studies abound, but I believe there are still many aspects of past-life research that need to be investigated. This has been my prime goal in writing this book.

While looking back at our previous lives can be exciting and enlightening, it is essential to remember that the answers we are seeking for this life can only truly be found by living in the present and releasing our past. It is also important to approach the whole area of past-life regression in a meaningful way. Deciding to explore our past lives is far from being some entertaining experience or a visit to a time tunnel Hollywood-style movie. The prime purpose is to look to the past to see what we can learn from it, always being mindful that the life that matters most is the one we are living now. These deeply buried memories properly approached could well be the key to the next stage of our development as a soul.

Past experiences play an ongoing role in everyone's life even though we often don't give them much thought. If you had a nasty experience with a dog as a child you may not react well to dogs as an adult and even have a deep, ongoing fear of being attacked again. You may even fear a dog coming near you. However, if it became a real problem then there are several avenues you may choose to explore to get over this phobia.

It's much the same principle for unresolved issues from past lives that need to be cleared in this lifetime. These issues can include everything imaginable, from our snapping canine friend through to deep emotional and physical wounds that have been brought back to be resolved along with the soul contacts associated with them.

The full history of our past lives is part of our soul energy and is buried deep in our subconscious mind. The best way I have found of unlocking these memories is to access the subconscious via deep hypnosis conducted by a reputable, experienced hypnotherapist. However, the subconscious also has various ways of alerting us about our past when the occasion demands. Just as we communicate with spirits in the afterlife in the dream state, we can be given clues in our dreams by our spirit guides.

It is also possible to tune in to past lives by going into deep meditation after expressing the intention of seeking answers to a current problem or situation. This I have found is more likely to happen with those who have been meditating regularly for some time. The caution here is that your visualisation may not always be that of a past life, but something you have conjured up with your subconscious mind as an answer to your question. If the answer is relevant and helpful, does it really matter?

I have always had a fascination with ancient Egypt and also the history of Rome, so it came as no surprise when a medium I was referred to told me about a lifetime I'd had as a Roman soldier stationed in Egypt that directly related to and explained a life-changing situation I was experiencing in my personal life. When visiting Cairo a few months earlier for the first time with two friends, both tour guides, I felt as if my life was in immediate and constant danger even though there was no obvious reason. This feeling faded after a few days and I soon forgot about it. The medium went on to inform me, with no prompting on my behalf, that I had been murdered, as she put it, 'in the shadows of the Pyramids'. She warned me that unless I made certain changes the person responsible would be the cause of my death in this lifetime. I had been careful not to mention to her that I had just visited both Egypt and Rome, nor indicated any interest in their history. Needless to say, I heeded the advice that she passed on from the spirit world.

There are many catalysts that can inspire us to seek answers from our past. Once the decision to investigate past lives is made for the right reasons it's often the first step to uncovering who we really are and what our purpose is in this lifetime. As I have written in my previous books, we are all spiritual energies having a human experience or, more correctly, a full range of human experiences.

And it certainly takes more than one lifetime to achieve that goal.

'Life on Earth is but a fleeting illusion edged between lives past and future, beyond physical mortal reality.' — George Harrison, former member of the Beatles

Chapter 3

A LIFETIME IN ANCIENT GREECE

The day was hot, with an unrelenting afternoon sun beating down on the twin columns of soldiers as they march resolutely through the barren hills. The centurion leading the small force of legionnaires sits comfortably astride his sturdy chestnut-coloured horse as it picks its way carefully along the stony path.

Walking behind the centurion, a tall, thin man brushes his dark wavy hair from a face more accustomed to the comforts of city life. His bare head and long, flowing, pale, dust-covered clothing makes him stand out from the Roman soldiers all too obviously dressed for battle.

Kasos, a Greek academic, is feeling decidedly isolated and increasingly uncomfortable as the tension grows in the ranks of the soldiers surrounding him. They are nearing the area in the hills that had been the scene of recent unrest by local villagers who want to free themselves from the yoke of Roman control with its heavy taxes. After days of unaccustomed walking at a military pace, Kasos now uses the staff he carries as the sign of his status purely as support for his tired legs.

No longer do the soldiers call out, teasing him with their

nickname for him of 'Alexander the Great'. Their normal jocularity has faded into a quiet, determined advance. While these jibes were made in good spirit, he is uncomfortable being compared with the military general of Greece's days of glory. Kasos is a man of peace and learning.

The year is 41 BCE, some 45 years after the Roman general Sulla sacked the city of Athens and slaughtered many of the population, bringing to an end any further ideas of revolt by the Greek people against the control of Rome. However, occasional small uprisings in outlying villages sting the Roman administration into action to keep the peace and let the inhabitants know who is in charge.

As he walks behind the centurion, whose flowing red cape keeps pulling his focus as it seems to draw him inexorably towards the violence he abhors, Kasos' mind drifts back to his early days. His family own a small vineyard near Athens that also grows olives, both crops a staple part of the Greek diet. His ancestors originally came from a small island near Crete, and although they are not in the wealthy class, as a boy growing up in a loving family he lacked for nothing.

Kasos was always destined for the life of a scholar and not a farmer, and his father, realising this, took him to a small academy of learning situated in the hills just outside Athens. It was 54 BCE and Kasos was twelve years of age. The master of the academy selected only six students for his class, and Kasos was offered one of the positions. Based on the teachings of Plato, this was a smaller offshoot of the famous philosopher's original academy located in north-west Athens.

In the years that followed Kasos studied philosophy and several languages, including Latin. Greece had been a province of Rome for many years, and by then Athens was a thriving multicultural city where the traditional learning of Greek scholars and artists was highly regarded by the Romans. Graduates of these academies were widely respected, and although only in his late twenties Kasos had already earned a reputation as the 'wise one' when he was 'selected' to help in this military campaign. He is conversant in certain local dialects and familiar with the area where the uprisings were taking place, and the Roman governor believed his status as a man of learning would help him communicate with the 'mountain people', preventing any further trouble. The governor wanted to understand the motives behind the unrest and believed the locals would open up to Kasos more than they would to the Romans.

Kasos chose to continue studying after he graduated from the academy, and also started to teach and help others. He was hoping to travel to broaden his knowledge; however, he had little money and needed a mentor. Perhaps, he thought, the Roman governor would help him after this campaign.

His main concern is that he too does not completely trust the Romans, who are still regarded by many of his countrymen as invaders. Roman rule is a blend of peaceful administration combined with harsh measures when necessary to maintain law and order. Kasos keeps reminding himself that the Romans do respect learning and the wisdom of the Greek scholars. The governor is also a friend of the master of the academy, so Kasos must tread warily.

The governor always calls the master Atticus, which is not his

Greek name. The Romans often give Greeks Latin names, whether they want them or not. Kasos reflects that it is their way of letting us know they control us.

Kasos' mind is jerked back to the present moment as the Roman centurion calls a halt and informs his troops they are getting close to the village and to maintain a strict watch. The village is in the hills near the old capital of Sparta, now in decline. Some local villages have tried to rekindle a part of the fighting spirit of the ancient Spartans, but the Romans are normally able to keep them under control.

Suddenly an avalanche of rocks and spears rains down on the lines of the legionnaires, who immediately form themselves into groups of testudo (or tortoise) by placing their shields over their heads in traditional defensive formation, making it appear like the shell of a tortoise.

Once the initial attack is thwarted the Romans go on the attack and the slaughter begins. Kasos is pushed aside as the soldiers methodically slay everyone in sight, women and children as well as the men who attacked them. They show no mercy as they lay waste to the entire village.

Kasos can only watch on sadly, his mission a complete failure. These are not his people, but they are his countrymen and this is a senseless loss of life. He knows that despite the Romans being prepared to settle the matter peacefully, the result was like stirring up a hornet's nest. Once disturbed the hornets go into a frenzy, stinging everybody in sight.

Standing in the middle of the carnage, the centurion calls Kasos to him and tells him that he must take the message back to as many people as possible that resistance to Rome is futile.

His heart heavy with sadness, Kasos can only nod resignedly.

The aftermath of the battle

Now back home in Athens, Kasos bears the emotional scars of the massacre of the villagers. He is no longer of any use to the Romans, who leave him to get on with the rest of his life.

The governor spreads word of the revolt, maintaining his troops were blameless and that they were attacked and simply defended themselves. Kasos meets with some of his former colleagues at the academy, as he feels the need to share the real story. He accepts there is a certain truth to the official story, but knows in his heart that the soldiers did not have to be so ruthless in their retaliation. Despite their friendliness to him, he knows that brutality is in their very nature and it does not take a lot to bring it to the surface. They tolerate no resistance, and the message to other potential troublemakers has to be very clear.

When he relates the true story of the massacre his colleagues shake their heads, saying, what else can we expect from these people? The Romans have been in control of Greece for many generations, and Kasos and his colleagues cannot even imagine what it must have been like in the glory days of Greece. They all admit that in many ways Rome has brought stability and economic progress to the crumbling Greek civilisation. Their studies have revealed the complacency and corruption that had brought their country to its knees. They have discussed the fact many times that democracy was not the same as it was when it was first introduced many centuries ago.

Kasos and his friends all accept that the golden age of Greece has long since gone. He believes the Roman soldiers derisively called him Alexander the Great because they wanted to let him know that Greece is no longer great. Greece for them represents the past, and Rome is now both the present and the future. The Romans are fond of reminding the Greeks they are doing them a favour by making Greece a province. However, Kasos is quick to point out they are taking a lot of riches from his country, including slavery, which is regarded as a form of wealth in Roman society.

After leading a solitary life in Athens, Kasos decides to finally return home to his family's farm to see out the remainder of his life. His brother, who he has not seen for many years, has been running the farm since their father's death and welcomes Kasos home. He is even given his old bedroom where he grew up as a child, in what now seems like a past life.

Now in his fifties, Kasos is happy to help educate some of the young members of his family and the children of some of the farm workers. There are no schools in these outlying areas and his knowledge and wisdom is gratefully accepted. He helps them achieve a basic education, including learning some of the history of Greece, and encourages them to develop their Greek language skills.

Kasos is content to see out his life peacefully surrounded by the love and support of his family. In his sixtieth year, his strength failing, Kasos struggles with his breathing before finally slipping away. He feels a great sense of release as his soul departs this life, floating gently away from his physical body.

***

At this point the voice of Peter Smith, the past-life therapist taking me on a journey into my past, asks, 'Let it unfold, and tell me: what do you sense around you?' My recorded voice, sounding very surprised, replies, 'I have an image of an ear, a large ear. It's a feeling that I need to speak, to be listened to.'

Peter's voice gently asks me, 'Now Kasos is back in the energy of the afterlife, what is it that your soul wishes to share from the life just experienced?' After a pause, my soul replies, 'Harmony, the harmony that was so missing in this lifetime. When one country is dominated by another, [there is] the feeling of repression, of not being free, to be who you really are.'

My soul voice continues: 'On the whole we were treated fairly well, but it was our country, and we were never allowed to feel it was our country. They were doing us a favour, rescuing us from ourselves. We didn't want to be rescued, we were there long before Rome, but we let it go.'

When asked about the purpose of that lifetime, what it was that I (my soul) set out to achieve, the answer came without hesitation: 'To discover the importance of freedom, what it means, and to have the choices which are yours and not dictated by others ... To be part of a heritage, a long distant heritage not demeaned in any way ... To live a non-military life, because the Romans are all military based, whereas we were about knowledge, information, philosophy and humanity. In many ways the Romans lacked humanity; they were like machines in many ways, war machines. Not only in our country, but in every country [they occupied]. They didn't always understand or allow the people to be themselves, to respect their heritage, respect their skills. They wanted to stamp their own authority, everything had to be Roman.'

Peter's voice gently urged my soul to go deeper and across the lineage of every lifetime I have lived, and asked why it was important for me to see this particular lifetime. 'To respect each other, to understand that because we have a way of life that it is not necessarily the best, or the only way of life. There are many cultures, many belief systems, histories, attitudes, behavioural patterns. There is not one common behaviour pattern. That is what humanity is, a huge variety, and we need to learn to respect this. I need to learn to respect this.'

At this point, still deep in trance, I let out a long sigh as my subconscious ingested this statement.

Peter: 'Help me understand the message that needs to be offered to humanity as a result of this discovery.'

'Humanity is like a diamond: it has many facets, but each one of those facets makes up the whole. Humanity is not one single facet; it is just part of a network, a tapestry.'

Peter: 'What are the messages that Barry's book needs to convey?'

'We are all part of each facet, there is a little bit of us represented everywhere. We have no right to look down on another part of the world, another race, any other belief system. We are all part of this [the diamond] and we may well have been an integral part of all of these facets at some stage. Where we are at the moment is just one phase of our entire existence. We are here to explore the whole diamond, not just one little chip off it. It's like it's a one hundred carat diamond, and this lifetime is only one small part of one carat.'

Peter: 'What is it you'd like Barry to understand as it unfolds, what does this beautiful project mean to him?'

'That we don't blame any aspect of our past. We have all had good times and we have all had bad times, we've had many, many experiences, but it is all part of who we are. Without this we really wouldn't have any purpose.'

Peter: 'Tell me more about that.'

'Our purpose is to experience all that is.'

Peter: 'And what does this mean for us?'

'Eternity. There is no beginning, there is no end; we just are. We grow … [we] are just on an eternal journey.'

Peter: 'What are the key themes for Barry to concentrate on for the book? What is it that needs to be offered to those who will read this book?'

'Understanding … Understanding why we are here, where we have been, understanding our purpose, where we choose to go. Understanding our goals, our limitations, our strengths, understanding those around us, their opinions, the parts they play in our lives, and our place in theirs. Everybody has to come to their own understanding, that's why we are here.'

'Have you ever sensed that our soul is immortal and never dies?' Plato, The Republic

Chapter 4

A VISITOR IN THE NIGHT

In the chilly pre-dawn hours of Wednesday, 13 July 2016, I struggled into consciousness as a voice from somewhere — who knows where — told me to wake up and take notes.

'Notes, what notes?' I grumbled. Switching on the bedside lamp, I looked bleary eyed at my watch; it was just after three in the morning. The room was freezing, it was mid-winter, and an involuntary shudder passed through me as I scrambled under the covers again.

The voice inside my head was insistent: 'Don't go back to sleep; you have work to do.'

This was not the first time I had been woken in this manner, though it was usually with answers to a problem that frustrated me. One contact I will never forget was the spirit of the ancient sixth-century BC Chinese philosopher Lao Tzu disturbing my sleep with the message I was to look for one of his insights for the answers I was seeking. I had never had any previous contact or even, to be honest, knew anything about this enigmatic figure. He identified himself, and I just knew somehow it was not a dream and I had to take notice.

I was soon able to get back to sleep, but woke the next morning wondering if it really had all been a dream. I looked at sayings of Lao Tzu, the founder of Taoism, on the internet but nothing felt right. A few days later my partner Anne had followed her intuition and found a quote that resonated with me. I knew intuitively it was the message I needed:

'*If you are depressed, you are living in the past. If you are anxious you are living in the future. If you are at peace you are living in the present.*'

It still gives me goose bumps, and I have been widely quoting that passage from Lao Tzu ever since.

However, on this cold winter's morning I knew there was no hope of just closing my eyes, as my inner voice would not let me rest until the message had been downloaded.

My thoughts over the previous couple of weeks had been turning over the idea of writing another book. My first two books were both doing well on the international scene, and my third book, *The Joy of Living: Postponing the Afterlife,* written with my partner Anne Morjanoff and my son Matt, was in the early stages of being published. I had been putting out the question that even though both books on the theme of life after death were popularly received was there still more to investigate, or had I done the theme to death? (Pun intended!) I had always felt that the first two books were part of a trilogy.

While researching and writing *Afterlife* and *No Goodbyes,* I had received a lot of help from a highly advanced spirit guide who simply wished to be known as M. So I presumed that it was M who had decided to give me a much-needed prod to get writing again.

Before I had a chance to ask if this was indeed my spiritual mentor, the soft but firm male-sounding voice in my head told me to get paper and a pen because he had a lot of information to impart. I flicked on the air conditioning for some much-needed warmth and tottered out to my office to get the necessary materials; I was soon propped up in bed, pen poised and ready to go. I looked at the pen I had randomly selected from my desk — it was one I had specially made for marketing *No Goodbyes* with its logo of the tree of life. 'Hmmm, a good sign,' I thought.

My guide didn't waste any time, and my pen started to fly across the page in what felt like automatic writing, a form of channelling that I sometimes still use. Here is what I wrote, word for word:

Life on Earth is similar to being an ex-pat, where you are on assignment to a foreign land far from home. You have accepted the contract for one of a thousand different reasons, and set off on a whole new direction.

You are leaving behind your loved ones, family, friends and your familiar environment. Everyone has a different background. Some are more experienced than others, some are young souls, others are well experienced, bringing their accumulated skills to their new life. There are fresh-faced, eager souls ready for new adventures, while others arrive with a whole lot of baggage from their previous activities.

Everyone has the same basic purpose, to leave the past behind, no matter what the circumstances, good, bad or indifferent, and look to new horizons. They are leaving behind the familiarity of their soul family, both close and extended (more on that later), and preparing to meet the new people they will encounter and work with in their next incarnation.

But do they have to do it alone? Unlike the ex-pat they are going to a place where people from their past, usually including some family members, will play an important role in their new adventures and experiences. While some members of their close soul families and friends may reincarnate in the same lifetime, many others remain in the world of spirit, or even reincarnate in other places and times.

Sometimes contact is established, and as with ex-pats, communication is maintained with those still at home. On Earth it is communication by telephone or internet, or even a quick visit, but for the reincarnating soul contact is usually of a spiritual nature. This is not always recognised unless there is outside help, such as a medium, or through dreams and intuition.

When their contract is completed the ex-pat usually goes home for a break before their next assignment. This new contract may take them to countries where they can work with different cultures and enjoy fresh experiences. Of course they may stay at home and use their experience in administration or management. When the ex-pat is ready to retire they will either return home or, depending on their circumstances, find another location where they can enjoy a chosen lifestyle. Their achievements and experiences up to the point of retirement will influence their future.

The incarnating soul has a very similar series of life experiences, spread over many lifetimes. The soul rests in the world of spirit in between lives before resuming their on-going contract. This may take countless lifetimes over thousands of years, but once completed the soul can head in several directions. It may elect to stay in the dimension of the afterlife, return to Earth in spirit form as a guide, or head off into lives in other worlds. Each soul's journey and ultimate destination is unique, depending on the experiences in the earthly lives lived and how it has evolved during its time on this planet.

The voice then faded and departed as quickly as it had arrived. I put the pen down and read what I had written; it felt as though I was reading it for the first time, and I knew the words had come from spirit. Afterwards it took me a long time to get back to sleep, which was hardly surprising given the circumstances. When sleep finally overtook me it was deep and dreamless, and thinking back after I woke I felt that my soul was processing this download of information. I re-read the words and was struck by the simplicity of the message and its meaning. It embraced a concept that I had explored in my previous books: 'As above, so below.'

Chapter 5

A STRANGE TALE FROM AN ANCIENT DESERT KINGDOM

The whole area of past lives and reincarnation has always fascinated me; I can't really say for certain why that is. Possibly it's part of my purpose in this lifetime to investigate and write about the subject. My first encounter with past-life exploration came as a result of a newspaper feature story in 1980 about Peter Ramster and his work in this area. Peter, a well-known Sydney psychologist, had stumbled upon past-life connections when he took a patient into hypnotherapy and instructed her to go back to when the situation at hand had started.

He was amazed to find that without any prompting she went straight into a past life, which ultimately turned out to be the origin of her current condition. Peter later shared with me that at the time he was a sceptic about past lives and was startled by her regression. However, his patient's journey into the past proved to be the catalyst for her healing.

After reading this feature I booked an appointment with Peter, and nervously turned up for the appointment a few weeks later. He sat me down in a comfortable chair and started the regression process. I felt myself drifting away peacefully at first, but then had the feeling that I was losing control and about to topple backwards into a deep, dark hole. My eyes snapped open, my heart began pounding and that was the end of my first regression. At that time I was yet to discover the benefits of meditation.

Peter explained that everyone has a different reaction to hypnotherapy and it was nothing to be concerned about. However, I felt very disappointed and also somewhat embarrassed and took off like a startled fawn. 'That is the end of that', I thought.

My interest in past lives did stay with me, though, and several years later while watching Peter's TV documentary *The Reincarnation Experiments* (available on YouTube) my desire to explore further was rekindled. Being an avid reader, I soon found several books from internationally renowned writers such as Jungian psychologist Roger J. Woolger, PhD, who wrote *Other Lives, Other Selves*, and Dr Ian Stevenson, whose work with children and past lives has been universally recognised.

Dr Stevenson was a psychiatrist who worked at the University of Virginia School of Medicine for 50 years, was chair of the department of psychiatry from 1957 to 1967, the Carlson Professor of Psychiatry from 1967 to 2001 and a research professor of psychiatry from 2002 until his death in 2007. He chose to exclusively study children, as he reasoned they were unlikely to fabricate past-life memories. In total, Dr Stevenson studied some 3000 children who reported past-life memories, and wrote 14 books on the subject. In approximately 1200 of these cases, Dr Stevenson was able to objectively validate the child's past-life memories (https://bit.ly/2w9oOf3).

Dr Stevenson's research showed these children frequently had birthmarks that supposedly related to either their murder or the death they suffered in a previous life. This opened a whole new area of scientific studies that many subsequent authors and researchers have used in their own publications. Both Stevenson and Woolger proved to me very early in the piece that the scientific approach they had to past lives was enough to confirm my own beliefs.

I re-established contact with Peter Ramster in the late 1990s after launching *Celestial Powers*, a new radio show in Sydney with mind, body and spirit themes as well as alternative and complementary healing therapies. Peter opened up a whole world of past-life encounters and metaphysical experiences in his on-air appearances, and has been a regular guest on my radio programs ever since. We soon established a friendship and he privately elaborated on some of the famous cases he explored in his TV documentary *The Reincarnation Experiments* and also in his book *The Search for Lives Past* (currently out of print). In one instance the person regressed went back to a lifetime when the planet was first inhabited by visitors from another world. She recalled a life as one of the crew of a space craft that crashed on Earth and was unable to return home. The members of the crew realised they had to start a new life here and eventually inter-married with the early inhabitants of the planet. This raises all kinds of questions about the evolution of the human race, as this may well have been one of many such encounters with visitors from other worlds.

Hearing this story only served to further whet my appetite for this whole subject, and I started my own investigations and also my own hands-on case studies. By now I was dividing my time between being a radio broadcaster, a lecturer in radio journalism and a voice-over artist as well as doing consultations as an astrologer and psychic. A couple of clients wanted to find out how the past was affecting their life and asked me if I would regress them.

My voice had a hypnotic effect on many of the clients coming to me for a reading, and I soon found that I had a natural ability to help certain people slip into a deep meditative state to access their previous lives. I started with brief regressions, and when they proved very successful I was able to increase them into a full session. I was given some very sound professional advice on this procedure and combined it with spiritual guidance to carefully help people discover how their current lives were closely linked with the past.

Since then Peter Smith has furthered my training in this area by putting me through his Hypnoenergetics course, which he pioneered in Australia.

The next step occurred naturally and out of the blue when I was asked to do a group past-life regression for about 10 people. I realised that a true regression was an intense and personal therapeutic experience that would be very different in a group setting. This group session would have to take the form of a deep meditation rather than full-on regression.

By now I had established a technique of relaxing my clients and taking them deep inside themselves then, when I intuited they were ready, I would take them step by step to the past down a stairway and into a long tunnel. There were many doorways set into this tunnel and one of them would appeal, inviting each person to open that particular door and go inside. We would then explore this lifetime before leaving and climbing the stairs again to the present. The insights gained were always relevant to the person concerned, providing them with answers to the problems or situations they were facing at the time.

The challenge of taking a group tour of the past intrigued me. Would I be able to work with more than one person at a time, or would it be an embarrassing flop? Fully prepared for some members of the group to have some problems and draw a blank, I was both surprised and delighted to find they all had some form of past-life experience during the meditation. Some were more detailed and in depth than the others, but overall it was a success. The group discussion afterwards was fruitful, and it was a very positive experience for everyone concerned.

This was to be the first of many such group sessions I conducted, and it was extremely gratifying to see and hear how people were able to find answers from the past to help them in some way in this lifetime.

My biggest challenge came when I was asked to be a guest lecturer on back-to-back cruises on an international ship, the *Southern Cross*, for the Christmas and New Year Pacific Island cruises in 1995/96. Prior to the first cruise I had prepared several talks about astrology, psychic intuition and numerology and needed one more subject, so I decided to talk about past lives and reincarnation and to also include a group past-life meditation. Once on board, the cruise director put me in the ship's library for the first talk as he expected only about 20 or 30 people would show up. To everyone's amazement the room was packed solid with about 60 people and many others were turned away, much to their disappointment.

After that it was decided I would relocate to the ship's theatre, as it was the only other space available. Thinking I'd be delighted if my talks could even half fill the 250 seat auditorium the next day, a big surprise was in store. Word had obviously spread and we got a near full house!

By the time we got to the past-life session the theatre was packed, with people even sitting on the stairs. Going on stage and looking at this sea of expectant faces did make my heart skip a few beats. I silently asked my spirit guides for their support and after the initial talk I went into the meditation sequence, hoping that at least some of the audience would be able to access their past in some way.

My guides must have been working overtime and also called in some extra help, because it was a roaring success and the feedback I received on stage and later in the cruise from the passengers was wonderful. One woman came to tell me her husband had always been fascinated with time, and when he went into a past life he saw himself as an old-fashioned watchmaker in London in 1878 working with intricate precision in making and repairing watches and clocks of all descriptions. Another man buttonholed me later in the cruise to say his wife had to drag him to the talk as he was a total sceptic. The lifetime he visited was so helpful to him in resolving a current personal situation that he was amazed and was now a total believer.

I was delighted at the response to such a large audience regression, particularly as the session was interrupted when the captain decided to do a test of the ship's alarm bells, which brought everybody back to earth with a jolt. Fortunately it was almost at the end of the regression and nobody in the audience seemed to have been unduly upset or disturbed.

A fascinating thing happened as I was finishing writing this book and in the throes of moving house. A 1996 magazine called *Highest Aspirations* just *happened* to fall from the front of an old book as I was sorting my library. I had no memory of this little magazine at all and wondered why I would even want to hang on to it. While leafing through the pages, much to my surprise I came across an article called 'Past Lives, Fact or Imagination?' I got an even greater surprise when I saw the author was one Barry Eaton! As I am a believer in synchronicity rather than coincidence, I naturally sat down to read the article.

It was the story of my past-lives presentation aboard the *Southern Cross* in 1995/96. I was delighted to see that the words I had already written in this chapter were an accurate reflection of my talk and demonstration. There was, however, another person's story that had slipped my mind, and which I am able to include now in this chapter. I have reprinted the paragraph verbatim:

The success rate of the regressions absolutely delighted me. The audience of around 250 people for each session produced some extraordinary past life experiences. There was the woman who spoke to me after one session who told of being hanged in the life she visited. Her neck was apparently broken by the hangman's rope. She then related how she has always suffered pain in that exact same spot all her current life. She said that she had been in pain that day, but the pain went after that session.

The second cruise went over just as successfully, with full houses and fortunately no alarm bell interruptions. After the past-life session several people came to talk to me, including a woman who waited around until the others left. Expecting another past-life recollection, I was delighted instead to learn she was clairvoyant and had seen many spirit helpers surrounding me on stage during the entire presentation. This confirmed for me just how much support I was receiving from spirit.

Following the cruise, I conducted a small group meditation for some passengers who were at my presentations and wanted a more personal experience. They were all keen to see what would happen, and slipped easily into a state of deep meditation. The post-regression discussion as usual turned up some exciting evidence. The one that stands out in my memory is the man who shared with the group that he had been shown himself in a past life as a young boy in rags who froze to death on the cobblestones of an old European city, which he thought may have been Paris. His wife then explained that in this lifetime he had always had a problem keeping warm, and at the time was wearing a pullover despite the fact it was a warm summer day. This regression was enough to explain to him the reason for his seemingly irrational inability to stay warm. His broad smile was an indication of the success of the exercise.

There was no way either of us could prove that he was that boy, but as an exercise in healing it was enough to help him change his life.

***

In the September following the cruise I was surprised to receive a letter from Gerard Benjamin, a passenger on board who had attended my presentations but had not made contact at the time. Gerard had written a short story for submission to a contest run by a national newspaper that year. Gerard enclosed a copy of his story for me, which he entitled 'Ancient History Now'.

His letter went on to say: 'Sincere thanks for the part you played in kick-starting a recollection which has proved to have been of inestimable significance, even more than the cruise itself. From the awareness gained by visiting a past life, I have developed a previously undiscovered ability to influence what happens to me in the future, by discovering a fuller understanding of who I am, and what my current life expects of me.'

I contacted Gerard at the time and he gave me permission to use his short story as part of my ongoing research into past lives. I read the story on air in one of my very early radio programs, but now am pleased to be able to reprint it here in full:

That was ancient history now, yet it's relevant to recall what I 'saw' on the 'Southern Cross'. Day seven's program for the cruise advertised a session on 'Past

Lives' convened by a Sydney radio personality. Sated with the food and excitement above decks, we arrived in the dimly-lit Ships Theatrette. Gloria said, 'this'll be good!' and good it was. 'Enough of the theory,' said the presenter after half an hour. 'Now it's your chance to experience what I've been talking about.'

The presenter's voice was deeply hypnotic and before long I was relaxing my hold on critical detachment. 'See yourself going along a dark corridor with many doors,' toned the presenter. 'Choose a door, look at the date on the door, and enter ...' he continued, and eventually I surrendered to the moment.

A remarkable thing happened. Deep in the meditative reverie, the 'door' I opened was dated 632, and the name that occurred to me was 'Petra'. While one part of my mind knew of Petra as an ancient city in the Jordanian desert, another part of me observed a strange scene.

There was sand and camels – lots of them. It was a caravan! A long line of heavily-laden animals, accompanied by a colourful collection of people, was about to move off. I wasn't part of it, more likely having something to do with checking its progress. I 'saw' myself as a man of about 24 years, darkly tanned and shrouded from head to toe in Arab garb.

Standing with me, watching the caravan's intense

activity, was my mother. My father was also there, he had some important local position. He was remonstrating insistently with a man who seemed to be the caravan leader. It was as if he were giving directions, first pointing to a chart, then to the desert, then back to the chart again.

The head man nodded as if he were trying to take all this in, and a curious incident followed. As a final gesture, my father proffered the small chart, but almost impatiently the head man waved it away as if to say, 'I don't need it.' At this point he seemed to lose interest in all this instruction, and stepped several paces to where my mother was standing.

Dressed in purple with gold thread braiding, she acknowledged his respectful greeting. He hesitantly said something like, 'may Allah bless us on our journey,' and her reply indicated that they would arrive safely. His craggy face broke into a wide grin and he clasped my mother's hand in gratitude.

My father witnessed this with absolute stupefaction. His face, an open book, reddened with rage. 'Look!' he must have insisted to himself, 'I've just told this man everything he needs to know about his journey – it's my job, for God's sake – and here, you say one prophetic word, and he's happy!'

He glared at my mother as if to blame her, yet didn't speak a word. She silently bore his contempt and stared out into the desert. It seemed as if this scenario had taken place between them before in many different forms, but this time it was the 'straw that broke the camel's back'. My father turned abruptly and walked away. This was the last time that I ever saw him.

My mother and I stood together knowing that something catastrophic had taken place, yet remained outwardly impassive. The caravan moved off and people waved to us in farewell, quite unaware of the little drama in which we had participated.

For the first time I was aware of a little girl behind us, sobbing her heart out. This was my sister, who had witnessed the whole scene and felt the venom of my father's reaction. Now she was expressing the desolation we all felt …

***

An emergency drill alarm abruptly rocketed everyone back to real time. Later, Gloria asked, 'where did you go?' and I told her every detail of the 'vision', to the point of calling her 'Mum'. In her present incarnation, her faith is strong and people, including me, have confidence in her word. When I made a momentous occupational change from lecturing to graphic arts, she was like a 'midwife' as I made the transition.

This Petra 'vision' had an eerie quality about it, much as a profound dream has. I wondered to myself, that if Gloria featured in it, might there be other people I knew who played a part in that scene? It wasn't long before that rumination proved affirmative.

An air traffic controller for who we had produced some charts often dropped in for a chat. Once he said that he had just returned from an overseas conference. 'Anywhere exciting?' we asked. 'Jerusalem, but I didn't spend much time there. I was more interested in the desert,' he said. 'In fact we set off in a taxi for a day trip, but got caught in a sandstorm.'

'Where were you heading?' I asked. 'Petra,' he said. Gloria and I almost fell off our chairs. Obviously this was my 'father' from Petra! Controlling airspace must surely be akin to directing caravans! Despite his penchant for a chat he did exhibit an abrupt disposition. On one visit, we loaned him some travel books and as he left he said, 'See you in a few weeks.' That was 18 months ago.

One day, as 'dad' was saying goodbye, he almost ran into Christine, a teacher for whom we also produce artwork, and this coincidence was a clue to me that she WAS my 'sister'. Apart from the fact that I have a real-life sister of the same name, Christine's job is to travel around the state in a station wagon, visiting schools, addressing meetings and dispensing instructional materials. In fact she had engaged a caravan builder to fit out her vehicle so that she could open the rear hatch, quickly pull out panels and produce an instant display. She even reported a dream to us whereby she wanted to invite Gloria to her 'caravan' but felt embarrassed about its untidiness. The clincher came when she told us that her daughter was resigning from the Air Force and was applying for a job as an air traffic controller!

Recently a new customer walked in who had all the characteristics of being a 'camel whisperer'. Tall, commanding and rough around the edges, he told us that he was an ex-master mariner turned film maker. Immediately, he and I both knew that we had met somewhere before, and we actually found that we knew people in common, yet absences from the country in pertinent years meant that we could never have met in those circles. Here surely was the 'caravan leader' once in charge of 'ships of the desert'! The mutual spark of recognition must have originated from 'Petra' days. He had strong ideas about what he wanted in his artwork, but deferred to Gloria's skill to add the final touches.

There are many more coincidences to lend credence to the fact that these particular characters are alive and well in my life today. Suffice it to say that these days, when someone says, 'haven't we met before?' I am inclined to answer, 'yes, but that is ancient history now.'

The short story had been hidden away in a folder for many years, and was another little gem that emerged as I was preparing to move house in December 2017. It was almost as if some unseen helper wanted to make sure it emerged in time to be included in this book.

While Gerard's conclusions about links with those people in his current life must be taken at face value, his story is another potential piece in the puzzle of previous lives and their relevance to our current life. Other events in the years following the cruise could well be the main reason for his past-life recall on the *Southern Cross* in 1995.

I managed to track down Gerard and we had a very enjoyable conversation. It turns out that not long after the cruise he and his partner Gloria decided to start a publishing company and named it 'GG Publishing Remembering the Past'. In the early days of their new business Gerard's research of his family roots took him to Shropshire to investigate connections in 19th-century England. Back in Australia, the link eventually led him to discover a 600-page notebook of faded copperplate script in Melbourne. It proved to be *Tom Hurstbourne: or A Squatter's Life*, written by John Clavering Wood, who turned out to be Gerard's great-great-grandfather. Written in 1865, it was later confirmed to be the second novel ever published in the state of Queensland. Gerard and his partner Gloria republished the book in 2010, and it was hailed by many literary experts and by one historian in particular as a potential best seller.

Sadly Gloria passed in 2011, but Gerard is still publishing historical works and family memoirs. Is it too much to suggest that the past-life regression that Gerard and Gloria had in December 1995 was the catalyst for their future exploration of his family history?

For me the answer is obvious.

Chapter 6

PAST LIVES, REINCARNATION AND THE AFTERLIFE

Many people will dismiss past-life regression as the subconscious merely creating a vision that is relevant to the person and their current situation. I am quite prepared to believe this is true in some cases, but over the years extensive past-life research in various parts of the world has been able to prove a link with previous lives. Names, dates and places can often be confirmed with no other possible explanation than a direct connection with another lifetime.

Luke R, a young boy from Ohio in the United States, kept telling his parents he remembered being killed in a fire in a previous life. He saw himself in flashbacks as a 30-year-old black woman named Pam from Chicago who jumped from a burning building and was killed. Luke often said things like, 'When I was a girl I had black hair', and also remembered the moment of his death as well as his rebirth when he was 'pushed back down to Earth'.

Investigations made for a documentary film revealed that a woman named Pamela Robinson had indeed died following a fire at the Paxton Hotel in Chicago in 1993. To add further proof, Luke was shown several pictures of different women about the same age as Pamela and successfully identified her photograph.

I conducted a spiritual development group in Sydney for 10 years and we occasionally did a past-life regression as part of the program. I took the group members into a deep state of meditation and then down a tunnel with many doors along the way. They were asked to enter a door to a lifetime they intuitively felt would provide answers for something that was relevant to their current life. Afterwards they were invited to share their experiences with the other members of the group. The group had varying degrees of success with messages from the past, but they all had at least glimpses into a past incarnation.

One of the group members, Gerri, shared a very vivid vision after one of our regressions. Gerri told the group she had revisited a life as a young woman living in a tranquil town in mediaeval England. She saw herself in a horse-drawn carriage in which she was heading to a castle to meet who she described as her 'knight in shining armour'. However, as she crossed the drawbridge leading into the castle it suddenly collapsed and her carriage toppled into the moat. She was trapped inside the carriage and unable to get out and drowned.

Gerri then revealed that during her current life she had huge difficulty crossing bridges and also going through tunnels. She was even nervous driving over the Sydney Harbour Bridge and only did so when it was absolutely necessary.

When sharing her vision with the group Gerri was quite disturbed by these images, but after she calmed down she realised this was the explanation she had been searching for to explain her phobia of crossing bridges. A few weeks later Gerri was delighted to tell the group she had been able to happily drive over the Sydney Harbour Bridge with no side effects, and was convinced she had put her fears behind her. Several years later she told me she had also conquered her fear of tunnels and recently drove through a newly constructed road tunnel in Sydney.

This indicates to me that sometimes healing can happen at various times after a regression and in different ways; there does not always have to be an instant answer provided. The soul, or perhaps our guides, may consider we need time to digest the information from the life just visited.

In another regression as part of a healing group in December 2001, Gerri initially found herself in a village square in what she described as a European town. She shared the vivid memories of this past life.

> Now I am standing at a large wooden table in a large, light room of my home. I'm wearing a long skirt and blouse, not a peasant or upper class one but somewhere in between. I have a sudden sense of wonderful well-being and happiness and I am now in my garden picking flowers and herbs, and putting them in my large, flattish basket.
>
> People would come to me in my home for help with health problems, and I also went out to help others in their homes.

Gerri was then taken into the future, where she saw herself in bed in a bright, sunny room that overlooked the garden. She had a male companion with her and some pets in the room. 'I feel very peaceful … now I feel a great restriction across my body … and now I feel peaceful again.' As she left this life to return to the present, Gerri passed through a wooden door into which had been carved '1874, Avignon'.

Some people are able to slip into past lives easier than others, and Gerri has proved to be a very good subject. With a few other demons to conquer, she visited past-life regressionist Kathryn Hand at the recommendation of me and my partner Anne Morjanoff (also my co-writer of *The Joy of Living*, Rockpool Publishing, 2017). We had worked with Kathryn at the first three Australian Afterlife Explorers Conferences and knew she was a genuine, caring and talented regressionist. Kathryn was also trained by Peter Smith. Kathryn's session notes put this into perspective.

'Geraldine had suffered with claustrophobia as long as she could remember. Driving through tunnels, using lifts or getting into confined spaces were things she had learnt to avoid for a long time. However, motived by the desire to fly to Spain to attend her son's wedding, Geraldine hoped that by discovering the source of this problem, she could cope with 21 hours in the confinement of an airline cabin. She came to see me in the hope that I could help her recover deep hidden memories of when this fear began.'

Gerri recounts her experience when taken back to a relevant past life.

I am Cecilia, the eldest child, living with my family in a castle in England. I am doing some needlework while my younger siblings play. I don't see a lot of my parents; my father is out with men fighting wars to protect our castle. My mother talks a lot with other women, her sisters and the nannies of the children.

Now at age 30 and too old to be looked after any longer, I want to go out into the world but I am told it's not safe. I am only allowed to wander in the countryside close to the castle. However, out here I feel freedom among the animals and the plants. I feel physically restrained within the castle and also, being the eldest, I am expected to look after the young ones, which is too much responsibility for me.

When I heard talk of marrying me off I decided to leave the family and enter the monastery and become a nun. This feels right, and I am now in a brown habit, black shoes and a high white hat with a scarf. Here I am able to tend the monastery garden, and my love of plants begins to grow.

I knew how to grow and tend the plants, which herbs and flowers to pick for the kitchen and for healing and how to make mixtures and tinctures for healing. I learned all this from my family and my family before that. [*sic*] The knowledge was passed down from generation to generation.

I was later sent to a monastery in France when they

needed someone to look after their garden. When they realised I had an aptitude for using plants to help people, I was allowed to do this too.

Now I enjoy a peaceful existence, being happy in the garden and helping people with health problems.

Unfortunately Cecilia's life of peace and harmony was turned upside down at the age of 50 when she was accused of harming someone when she treated them with herbs. She was put in prison in the nearby town and put on trial, accused of being a witch. The authorities were ignorant of the healing power of plants and reasoned that she was using magic.

Cecilia recalls the final hours of her life. 'The prison cell is dark and cold, with only a little light coming in from a small window. I feel cold and very despondent.'

She next finds herself standing amidst noisy confusion on a platform in the town square, surrounded by a gathering of townspeople who have come to see her hanged. 'I look around and see the hangman and the rope behind me. I am terrified as the people are cheering, baying for my blood; it makes no difference that I am a nun. I have lost all hope now.

I am trying to keep calm inside and pray. Then I hear a loud roar from the crowd and feel a restriction in my throat, then everything goes black. Finally, I have the sensation of floating up and away from all the noise, and a sense of freedom.'

Gerri felt that after she visited her life as a nun she was able to take a lot of pressure out of her current life in the months that followed. Gerri has always enjoyed a great love of gardening and spent many hours tending her garden with its wide variety of plants. She is also a great believer in the power of herbs, and before she retired worked as a healer in addition to her corporate work. Gerri has not felt the need to use her skills as a healer since the regression, so she may well have released any past associations and is now able to move on to another phase of her life.

Although she did not recognise any other people from her life as a nun, Gerri does recall feeling very distant from her parents and siblings. This could indicate there was no soul family connection, and Gerri agrees it would explain why she was prepared to enter a monastery just to get away from them. There are many such stories about the benefits of exploring past lives, and this is now becoming more widely accepted by the public as well as many practitioners as a valuable therapy.

'The past has no power to stop you from being present now. Only your grievance about the past can do that. What is grievance? The baggage of old thought and emotion.' — Ancient Chinese philosopher Lao Tzu

Past-life research is usually regarded as simply tuning into previous lives from our current perspective to provide answers to ongoing problems. Most past-life therapists and researchers believe the primary reason for exploring past lives is to learn from previous experiences with the intention of clearing karma that is creating obstacles in this life. These blockages may be emotional, mental or physical, and prevent us from enjoying and fully participating in life.

However, I believe it is important to delve much deeper into the whole area of past lives and reincarnation to find reasons rather than just treating the symptoms. Past-life regression is a very powerful therapy that has helped countless people around the globe, myself included. There are many case studies available that prove beyond reasonable doubt we all do live many lives, but regression is just the tip of a large iceberg.

To fully understand and embrace this whole subject we first need to accept the existence of an afterlife. It's important to move beyond the notion that the physical body is the be all and end all of life, as most people seem happy to believe. We are, in fact, a spiritual energy that uses a physical body as a vehicle to have an earthly experience. When that body dies the energy that is the soul has to go somewhere, as energy cannot be destroyed but it can be transmuted. Logically the soul returns to its point of origin: call that the afterlife, heaven, the world of spirit, the universe or whatever label you choose.

Having already written two books about the afterlife as the real home of the spirit (*Afterlife: Uncovering the Secrets of Life After Death* and *No Goodbyes: Insights from the Heaven World*), I fully accept that we return there for a period of rest, recuperation and further learning before undertaking the next step in the evolution of our soul. This may entail reincarnation on Earth, or perhaps some other world, while some advanced spirits may have evolved sufficiently to remain in the world of spirit as they have completed their reincarnation cycle.

A word of explanation: the soul is that everlasting, indestructible energy that is our true essence, and the spirit is the vehicle that it uses to protect and attach itself to the body at the heart. The soul is a tiny fragment of the source or creative force that we label as God.

Ancient references to reincarnation can be traced to India and Hinduism as far back as the ninth century BC. It was then adopted by religions such as Buddhism and Jainism before being embraced by Chinese Taoism around the third century BC. It became part of Greek philosophy, notably Platonism, which stated that souls came from a celestial world and had to go through a series of reincarnations before returning to a state of pure being. Plato may have been influenced by the earlier philosophies of Pythagoras, who maintained the soul was immortal and after death went through a series of rebirths. In between each life the soul was purified in the underworld.

Indigenous tribes hold varying beliefs about reincarnation, some accepting while others do not embrace the belief. Australian historian and archaeologist Steven Strong, the author of *Out of Australia: Aborigines, the Dreamtime and the Dawn of the Human Race* along with Evan Strong, states that Australia's original people firmly embraced reincarnation, or the transmigration of souls as it is also known.

In an interview on my radio program *RadioOutThere* in 2017, Steven spoke about this belief as spirits being released from the body in a death ceremony so they could return to the tribe at a future time, bringing back all their accumulated knowledge and wisdom. They could also work on any unfinished business from their past life, which we now understand as karma. However, if a spirit was 'given freedom' by the tribe and told never to come back to country, it was like being cast out to wander lost in a kind of limbo for eternity. It was therefore vital to stay attached to the tribe, as this was essentially a spirit's ever-evolving soul family.

Today, major religions such as Buddhism, Taoism, Judaism and Hinduism all embrace reincarnation as an integral part of their beliefs. In the *Bhagavad Gita*, one of the most authoritative books of the Hindu religion and a part of the *Mah bh rata*, reincarnation is clearly stated as a natural process of life that has to be followed by any mortal. The most quoted text on reincarnation by Krishna says:

> Just as the self advances through childhood, youth and old age in its physical body, so it advances to another body after death. The wise person is not confused by this change called death. Just as the body casts off worn out clothes and puts on new ones, so the infinite, immortal self casts off worn out bodies and enters into new ones.

Certain Western belief systems think we go into a holding pattern in a sort of resting place after we die and presumably disappear into some kind of eternal hibernation, with the hope of resurrection at a future stage. Other religions flatly reject any form of ongoing life, believing we just fade away into blackness.

The 2008 European Values Study revealed that on average about 25 per cent of people across Europe accepted the concept of reincarnation. It is impossible to guess the current acceptance rate, but some estimates put the number of people who accept or embrace reincarnation in some form at around 25 per cent of the world's population, around 1.5 billion people.

For various reasons, reincarnation is refuted by all the main monotheistic religions of the world. Christianity has denied the possibility of reincarnation for many centuries, but it has not always been that way. Interestingly, reincarnation officially disappeared from early Christianity through the influence of Theodora, the wife of the Roman emperor Justinian. A former actress and prostitute, she managed to convince her much older husband to revoke all references to reincarnation as she believed it would prevent her from being recognised as a goddess. With the help of the Patriarch Mennas, Theodora convened the Synod of the Eastern Church of Constantinople in 543 AD and had reincarnation removed from the books (https://bit.ly/2OLJOjV). This proved to be the first death blow to the ongoing acceptance of reincarnation by the Christian Church.

Theodora died in 548, and for those who embrace the principle of transmigration of souls has more than likely reincarnated many times; only the Akashic Records could reveal where, when and how many times.

'Everybody dies, but nobody is dead.' — Old Tibetan saying

Chapter 7

SOUL FAMILIES AND PAST-LIFE CONNECTIONS

A significant part of my research into past lives comes from my contacts in the world of spirit. My abilities as a medium have been developing over the last 20 years or so, and I am privileged to work with a master guide and many spiritual helpers to explore this whole subject, which has always fascinated me.

I have also been working with Kelly Dale, a very gifted trance medium who channels, among others, the spirit of his father John Dingwall, a former Australian screenwriter and film producer best remembered for his film *Sunday Too Far Away.* John passed over in 2004 and was selected by the powers that be in the spiritual realm to communicate information and knowledge to people on the Earth plane. I knew John when he was here on Earth and have known and worked with Kelly for many years. The two are very different in manner, speech, wisdom and knowledge, and there is a marked difference when John communicates through his son.

John acts as a kind of mouthpiece for a large number of spirits at various levels in the afterlife. At last count it was around 100 spirits but this number has now increased significantly, providing an in-depth source of knowledge and experience as well as creating the energy necessary for communication from the afterlife.

Working with John, whom I refer to as my 'spokespirit', I have been able to learn a huge amount about that dimension we refer to as the afterlife, as well as the ongoing connection between spirits and life on earth. The guide who worked with me on my two books about the afterlife likened John's role to that of my previous work as a news reader. The public only sees or hears the news presenter, but there is a whole team behind the scenes reporting, writing and researching that information. Some of those team members pop up with special news reports, while others remain in the background.

John and I had not been in contact for some time because of commitments that Kelly and I have had in the last few years. When I told John my publishers had asked me to write a book about past lives, he broke into the familiar chuckle I have come to enjoy: 'Oh, have you?' he stated in a wry tone, which immediately told me he was expecting this new contact.

'Was there a little push from your side for that?' I enquired innocently. 'Well, let's just say I had a small hand in it,' he replied with another chuckle.

In previous communications John and I had briefly discussed the question of past lives and reincarnation, which are a given for both of us. However, we had not really spoken about the question of soul relationships to any great extent and I was keen to pursue this topic with him. It is popularly believed that your soul mate is your perfect partner, one with whom you have shared many previous lives with and then meet again to take up where you left off. Soul mates can come in many forms, though: partners, lovers, colleagues, friends and even antagonists. We have all agreed to meet up again to play out our combined karma via all kinds of relationships and scenarios. We all have a primary soul mate (*Destiny of Souls*, Michael Newton, Llewellyn Publications, 2000, pp. 263-4), who may incarnate as a partner, sibling, close friend and, of course, a love partner.

I skipped the preliminaries with John and got straight to the point, with a question that had been intriguing me for a while about soul mates and soul families: is everyone part of a soul group or family?

'Everyone has some form of soul connection; some are small and some are very large,' was John's reply. We had previously discussed what John refers to as a three-dimensional tapestry that links everyone in some shape or form, in this and other lifetimes. He went on to elaborate: 'The number of soul contacts we have is directly related to the amount of learning these connections have with each other.' Apparently it is not just a one-way street as we go through our soul experiences; we can oscillate between being a student in one life and the teacher in another. Even those spirits who have advanced to higher planes in the afterlife are learning from those in lower levels.

John explained: 'Soul families are all placed in groups to learn and evolve and then move into other groups. They will go on to move into the lives [on Earth] they were meant to, and these lives may be short or they may be long. The whole idea is evolution, learning and moving to a higher position which one attains by knowledge,' he concluded.

This came as a bit of a surprise to me, as I had assumed that when we were part of a soul group or family it was a fixed structure, just as our family is in life. The idea that soul families and groups are a moveable feast makes a lot of sense. It can be compared to the extended family situation that has now become such a normal part of life, with divorce, separation and various kinds of relationships affecting us all.

Connecting with my master guide while writing this book made me feel that I really needed to know a bit more about my own soul family in this lifetime. I went through a list of names of family and close friends and confirmed my soul connections and past-life relationships. That knowledge is private to me, but it has helped me understand various relationships and events during my life.

At the time of this research my partner Anne and I were dealing with the sad news about a friend in the UK, Mark, who had been given just weeks to live. Although we had only met in 2010, I felt a strong soul connection with him. I rang Mark as he rested at his home; we both knew this would be our last earthly contact. Mark had enjoyed his life to the full and then some, and was a highly spiritual man. Our conversation was fairly brief, and we agreed to meet up again in the afterlife to enjoy one of his famous banquets. After we shared a couple of quiet laughs it was time to say farewell, and we both broke down. Even now as I write these words I am fighting back the tears. I knew that Mark would transition to a much happier and pain-free life, but as Shakespeare wrote: 'Parting is such sweet sorrow.'

Each lifetime we experience on Earth is basically about the

development of our soul energy, which can take a long, long time according to my spokespirit John Dingwall. Some spirits were 'going to get it' sooner than others, just as humans do. For others, their destiny will lie in remaining in the world of spirit to teach, nurture and help others. John said this was a huge calling that not many spirits can do, and compared it to remaining celibate for your whole life on Earth. John describes this as a constantly evolving notion, as souls also do have the flexibility to request the areas to which they can go to learn and develop. Permission is given by the elders and guides in spirit if it fits that soul's destiny and its greater good.

I later asked my master guide if we can live hundreds or even thousands of lives here on Earth; he replied that there is no limit to how many lives we experience, that it is up to each individual soul. I was able to get a definite answer about my past lives when my guide told me that my current life is number sixty-six in my Earthly cycle. I believed at this time that I had not had a previous life on another world, so I put in an advance request for next time. I have not as yet received a reply. Maybe it's like a job application, and I'll just have to wait until management looks at my qualifications and makes its decision.

Another question often asked is whether there is a set period in between lives or whether it depends on the individual concerned. 'It could be ten years, or it could be twelve months [of Earth time]; it really depends on the individual. There has to be some time, as you can't finish a life and then move into another life the next day. There has to be a period of reflection, otherwise it's all rushed.'

That period of reflection will depend on each soul and what their future involves. This decision is not purely up to an individual; again, it is made in association with guides and elders who are directing that soul's path.

Has the Earth's ever-increasing population in the last hundred years or so affected the period in between lives? John confirmed there is 'some sense of urgency to move spirits along and get them back into their next life because of the dire nature of the situation on Earth. So spirits need to reflect on their last life, learn about the next one, move on and get cracking.' From this description of events in the between-life state it would appear that things have changed radically in recent years as more and more people are born.

In earlier conversations John confirmed that many souls from other worlds are also reincarnating on ours, and that these are seen as being very exciting times. John summarised the current situation in this way: 'Hopefully we can keep sending back spirits who have the right message in this time of need.'

John also confirmed information I included in my previous book *No Goodbyes*, that new souls are also being created to fill the need for Earth's burgeoning population. These souls hive off from older, more-advanced ones to start a whole new path for themselves.

John was very enigmatic when I enquired about how *much* choice we have in our next life. 'We have a lot of choice, and we have no choice.' He then explained that while we may have a lot of ideas about what we want in our next life, that doesn't make it appropriate or even what is considered best for us. 'We have several elders and higher spirits and [soul] brothers and sisters. Sometimes millions of souls can all have a say in the direction of one soul.'

This was a whole new ball game for me, as I had never countenanced the prospect of multiple souls being involved in our future life planning. Images were swirling in my mind of masses of people making these decisions in some sort of spiritual voting system, so I asked John how that works.

'It's as simple as thought communication,' John continued. 'If an advanced spirit puts out the call to help someone find their true path in the next life, you can have hundreds of thousands of souls all in effect meditating to the greater good of this one soul.' As there is no such concept as time in the afterlife, John explained that this can be an almost instantaneous energy source for that one soul. 'And it can be *whoomph*, firing like a laser, and that one soul can move on and move forth.'

This led to my next question: how does karma come into this equation? 'Karma can be created by one soul, yourself, and it can also be created by others for you to learn lessons.' He went on to say that we can go into a life where we help create our own destiny and karma. However, the choices we make in that lifetime may fly in the face of our good intentions and also our destiny. The karma we create by those actions can have a lasting effect for several lifetimes to come.

Karma maybe created by higher souls to give us lessons in our lifetime, but many people don't take advantage of this through questioning themselves and taking a positive direction to overcome the obstacles placed in front of them. Slow learners may take many lifetimes to deal with these issues so they are then able to move on to other experiences.

Another question that has intrigued me is about the planning that has to go into each life after it has been decided that certain people, such as parents, must be part of the karma. How is this framework planned, I have often wondered, as it involves an intricate pattern of souls on diverse paths and all born at different times and stages of our life? As usual, John and his team had the answer to hand.

So that all the pieces can fit together this life may have been created several lifetimes previously, depending on how many times we have come back to the afterlife and the karma we have created. This framework will also be put together by higher spirits who are connected to our development. As John summarised: 'It's all about learning, learning, learning and development, development, development. The object is to guide and inspire us to move on to the next stage of our soul development.'

Is there ever an end, I asked? 'Well, I have never found it,' was John's reply.

John admitted he is still carrying karma from issues involving guilt, loneliness, resentment and anger from previous lives. As an afterthought he also threw in happiness, so it wasn't all negative. He said his issue now is to turn these events into positives. In his group work in the afterlife John is questioning why he brought these behaviour patterns into each life. He freely admits he has not been learning his lessons, but is now working on ways to ensure he can put all this behind him in his next life and move on.

The difficulties we face in each life are from the tests spirit throws in our way through partners, sexual experiences, drugs, alcohol and the many forms of material temptations with which we are all familiar. 'Deep down we all know the truth, no matter how clouded our mind is; we always have a choice. The temptations are so great, the vast amount of us make the wrong choices.'

As someone who has cheerfully given in to many temptations in my life, John's words had a chilling message of truth. This is the kind of reality that is very hard for us all to face, let alone turn our backs on. When I raised the question of temptations around the ever-expanding world of technology, particularly in relation to the younger generation, John's reply said it all.

'There has never been a time in history when there has been so much temptation, and that is there for a reason. The dire situation of the planet and of the human race is so strong, it's as if these lessons need to be learned fast.' He went on to say that spirit doesn't have (Earth) time to put up one temptation at a time in front of people. They are bombarding them so they can learn their lessons as quickly as possible to be able to develop and move on in this lifetime.

This confirmed my belief that many members of the younger generation have reincarnated at this time to take the vital steps to help us survive the current crises and hopefully advance into a more peaceful and understanding world.

One guest on my radio program *RadioOutThere*, UFO expert Mary Rodwell, explores this theme in her book *The New Human:*

Awakening to Our Cosmic Heritage (New Mind Publishers, 2016). Mary investigates the question of a new generation, which she identifies as *starseed children*. She explains that these children, who are part of what is being described as the *millennials,* have incarnated to help raise humanity's consciousness beyond our limited 3D reality. The starseed children have experienced many lives on other worlds and are mostly incarnating on Earth for the first time, bringing their subconscious knowledge and experience to our world. During hypno-regression they recount stories about advanced instruction on other planets as they recall their past lives and experiences on a number of other worlds.

These children show that the whole concept of past lives and reincarnation is not limited to our earthly civilisation, but is understandably a universal occurrence.

Chapter 8

WHY WE CAN'T REMEMBER OUR PAST LIVES

This frequently asked question is a convenient excuse for sceptics to dismiss reincarnation and the existence of an afterlife as being just another New Age piece of fiction or a woo-woo mind game. My initial thought is: do the sceptics hate their lives so much that they can close their minds even further to the prospect of continuing life in some form? You would think that even a slight prospect of moving on to an afterlife, rather than having everything disappear into some kind of black void at the time of death, would at least be worth investigating and not merely dismissed out of hand.

I often feel sorry for close-minded cynics and sneering sceptics. One question they cannot answer with any credibility is: 'What is the purpose of a lifetime gathering knowledge, wisdom and unique experiences for it all to be ultimately snuffed out and dumped into a gigantic garbage grotto of blackness?' It relegates each individual to the status and importance of a slug (with apologies to the slug world).

Putting that aside, it still leaves us with the question of why even those who accept and embrace the concept of reincarnation can't consciously remember their past lives. Some can, as previously mentioned. There are many records of children recalling and telling vivid accounts of their immediate past life, but in many instances parents do not take them seriously. While past-life memories for children can be strong, they usually begin to fade out by six or seven years of age and soon disappear into the subconscious realms of the mind.

While children can cope with these flashes from previous existences, as they grow up it would interfere with their development in this life if these memories persisted. As adults we have so much new information coming into our daily lives that to add innumerable past-life memories to the conscious mix would be more than the vast majority of us could manage.

Just try to imagine the mental and emotional chaos we would create if recollections from all our lives were constantly crowding into our conscious minds — events from hundreds, maybe thousands of years ago triggering emotional, dramatic or catastrophic images and reactions whenever things go pear shaped. It's a daunting thought. Here you are in this life enjoying a social evening with some friends when WHAM!, out of the blue, a vision reveals that one of those friends in a past life deceived you, ran off with your partner and left you to die miserably in prison. Could you cope with such a memory and still stay civil, let alone enjoy their friendship? How would a child at school cope with the knowledge that their teacher was their worst enemy in a previous incarnation? What about a life lived on another world; how would that interfere with your daily activities if memories came crowding in at inopportune moments?

Unwanted past-life incursions starting in childhood and cropping up right through life would be enough to drive anyone around the bend. It would be nothing short of chaotic.

Sometimes people will have flashes of past-life images, whether it is in the conscious mind or the dream state. These flashes may come as a warning of impending danger or at a time of a major life lesson unfolding.

We need to start each incarnation afresh with the innocence of a newborn babe, not with a mind full of past memories and events. While our soul subconsciously contains the memories of all our lives, we are able to enter each incarnation with a clear, conscious mind to allow us to have the experiences necessary for our soul's evolution free from the baggage of the past. Happily, our soul always knows the purpose of our life, and if we tune in and listen to our inner wisdom it can help us stay on track. When the occasion demands, and with professional help, we are able to access the relevant past lives stored in our subconscious to help us overcome the karmic obstacles we face and move on in a positive manner.

Sir Arthur Conan Doyle, the famous author and creator of Sherlock Holmes and also a renowned spiritual researcher, is often quoted in a speech he gave on this issue: 'Such remembrances would enormously complicate our present life. Our existences may well form a cycle, which is all clear to us when we come to the end of it.' In other words, life is complex enough without the added confusion of past-life memories dogging our footsteps.

At the end of our lives, when the veil begins to lift, we can have greater clarity about the life we have lived and the lessons learned. In many cases this brings a great sense of peace for our transition to the afterlife.

'With reincarnation man is a dignified, immortal being, evolving towards a divinely glorious end; without it he is a tossing straw on the stream of chance circumstances, irresponsible for his actions, for his destiny.'
— Annie Besant, *The Ancient Wisdom*

Chapter 9

IS REINCARNATION INEVITABLE?

'Everyone who is seriously involved in the pursuit of science becomes convinced that a spirit is manifest in the laws of the universe – a spirit vastly superior to that of man.' — Albert Einstein

The general consensus seems to be that you can't prove reincarnation scientifically, but does that mean it doesn't exist? After all, science is also unable to prove the existence of love, and yet it is universally accepted as a vital human emotion. Where would we be without love in our lives if we abandoned it because it cannot be proven in a laboratory? So if past lives can't be relegated to a test tube examination the whole concept needs to be dismissed out of hand, right?

Wrong.

Let's look at the world of science. The word 'science' is defined in the Oxford Dictionary as 'an organised body of the knowledge that has been accumulated on a subject'. Other dictionaries give similar definitions. The very nature of their work means scientists normally focus on their own specialty area and rarely venture outside their circle of expertise.

There are many invaluable areas of expertise and applications in science, but its universal credibility as a collective source is not necessarily always justifiable, much less acceptable, by open-minded seekers of knowledge. Mainstream science has no real framework to explain non-materialist phenomena such as psychic abilities, intuition, paranormal activities, astrology and the existence of past lives. Surely impartial examination of the available evidence of these phenomena is warranted?

In a radio interview I conducted in 2016 with now retired US neuroscientist Dr Robert Davis, I asked him why strong evidence of past lives is widely rejected by scientists. Bob is very open minded about the whole subject and has written books about near-death experiences, the afterlife, consciousness and UFOs. 'Well, some scientists will say there is such a thing as genetic inheritance, the cellular memory,' he replied. I then pointed out that cellular memory is only related to the body, so how could that be influenced by a past life in another body, in a different location, in another time?

He went on to describe lab tests with mice that had aversions, for example, to smell. That learned behaviour was transmitted to their offspring, who then passed that aversion to other generations. From that it was deduced these experiences, including memories, can possibly be transmitted across successive generations. This was used as a scientific explanation for why human beings have learned experiences from their ancestors.

I pointed out the fallacy of this kind of testing for past-life memories. Those people, especially children, who have been investigated by such researchers as Dr Ian Stevenson described lives that were in no way related to their current family situation. Dr Davis was inclined to agree.

Dr Stevenson's research into reincarnation started in 1960 when he was chair of the Department of Psychiatry at the University of Virginia School of Medicine. He went on to write 14 books and authored 300 papers on reincarnation, and is recognised as one of the world's foremost authorities on the subject. His files contain over 3,000 case studies.

The following points are features of Dr Stevenson's work, which continued until his passing in 2007:

- Children start describing a previous lifetime as soon as they are able to speak, usually between the ages of two and three; these memories start to fade around the age of six or seven. They often tell their parents they have a different name, and that this family is not their true one. The other family lives in a different part of the world, but the child remembers names, locations and descriptions of such things as the house where they used to live.

- The child had a strong memory of their death in that lifetime, and in around 50 per cent of cases it was either a premature or violent death. Those who died of certain wounds would bear a birthmark or scar representing that fatal wound. In 35 per cent of cases Dr Stevenson investigated, children who died an unnatural death developed phobias in their current life related to that previous death. Families who decided to follow through on their child's information were able to eventually discover and contact the 'other family'. They were amazed to find that the child was able to recognise the members of the family and remember their circumstances, even such things as secrets or other information that only the family would know. The other family often then embraced the child as their reincarnated loved one and a new relationship started. The child's parents in the current life were often concerned they would be rejected, but that was not the case as the child was able to bond with both families.

- The child retained many personality traits from their previous incarnation, such as favourite foods or clothing, and also certain behaviours, which the other family was able to confirm.

- In a high percentage of cases researched by Dr Stevenson the sex of the child was the same as that of the past lifetime. However, some children who were members of the opposite sex in their previous life often had problems in adjusting to the new sex. This could lead to homosexuality later on in their lives. Girls reborn as boys, for example, may want to dress as girls or prefer more feminine pursuits.

- Many of the children with past-life memories showed abilities or talents they had in their previous lives. This is a possible explanation for child prodigies such as Wolfgang Amadeus Mozart, who composed his first work at the age of five and first performed in public at the Court of Bavaria just one year later. There is an impressive list of child

prodigies available on the internet (https://en.wikipedia.
org/wiki/List_of_child_prodigies); however, one young
boy stands out from the rest. Christian Heinrich Heineken
(1721–1725), a child prodigy also known as 'the infant
scholar of Lubeck', could speak from a very early age. By
the time of his death at four years of age, he was well versed
in mathematics, history and geography. He could speak
Latin and French in addition to German, his native tongue.

A discussion I had with John Dingwall confirmed the work of
such researchers as Dr Ian Stevenson, that a lot of children do
consciously remember their past life in the first few years of their
new incarnation. Whereas most children's memories of their past
fade at around seven years of age, John revealed this will change
in the near future. 'Those memories are going to last and linger
longer because of the dire situation the Earth is in, and this could
extend up to 10 or 11 years of age. It is difficult for children to
remain pure in their thoughts because there are so many obstacles
in the way.' While John chose not to elucidate on this, he has
spoken in past contacts about children growing up too quickly and
also about the effects of increasing dependence on technology on
their development.

I've noticed these days that children are being encouraged to
pursue so many interests and activities that the wonders of nature
and quiet contemplative time without technology are often no
longer part of their upbringing. Sadly, this makes it more difficult
to embrace what really resonates with their soul.

Sometimes a spirit even reincarnates for a very short life to play a role in their family's soul progress. 'There are so many lessons to be learned,' said John, 'and a lot of children leave life early, so the lesson is not so much for the child but for the grown-ups that surround them. Losing their child is almost the most powerful lesson a person can have.'

Dr Stevenson's work has inspired many other academically qualified experts such as Dr Michael Newton, Brian L. Weiss MD, Jungian psychotherapist Dr Roger Woolger and Australian psychologist Peter Ramster, who followed in Woolger's footsteps and has thoroughly investigated the subject of past lives.

Despite his academic background as a clinical psychologist, Peter Ramster maintains he was able to accept the existence of reincarnation because he has always kept an open mind in life. I have interviewed Peter many times and got to know him well, and I endorse his status as one of Australia's foremost experts on reincarnation.

In an appearance on *RadioOutThere* in August 2016, Peter recounted the story of one of his first case studies into past lives. He had a patient under hypnotherapy and told him to go back to when the problem started. His patient, a businessman having professional problems, went straight to a past life as a slave that was the catalyst for the problem. Peter laughed when he recounted the story, as he said when the man came out of trance he refused to believe what had happened. As Peter said, 'I was the one who believed him, even though he didn't believe himself!' However, his patient returned to that same life in a further five regressions, much to the man's amazement. The proof was in the pudding, as the old saying goes, because the patient's condition was completely healed following his past-life therapy. That event sparked Peter into looking more deeply into the potential effects of past-life memory.

Peter went on to produce two films entitled *The Reincarnation Experiments* (available on YouTube), which were shown by TV stations in many countries. As part of the film, Peter regressed several subjects who went back to past lives in the UK and Europe and revealed some amazingly detailed information. He then took the subjects overseas with a film crew, and they were able to verify the facts revealed under hypnosis. In one instance it was proved that one woman, Gwen, had never left Australia, yet under post-hypnotic suggestion she was able to unerringly guide Peter and the crew to a house near Glastonbury in England that she had visited as a child in the 18th century. Gwen had previously described the house in great detail, including the foundation tile on the floor she remembered when she went there with the owner, Mr Brown, after a childhood accident.

When Peter, Gwen and the crew arrived they found the building was now being used as a chicken shed and the floor was covered in dirt and chicken droppings. The bewildered farmer agreed to clean the floor and everyone was speechless when the tiles exactly matched the sketch Gwen had made in Australia, right down to the mason's signature mark.

Gwen had also described three stepping stones in a stream near the house, and said the middle one was wobbly as she remembered it as a child. They found the stream, but no sign of the stepping stones to which Gwen had taken them in her post-hypnotic state. However, Peter later met a local resident who had lived nearby all his life and he remembered the stones, right down to the wobbly one. They had been removed some 40 years previously.

If Peter had even the slightest doubts about Gwen's 18th-century lifetime this was the clincher, and even the film crew was convinced. Having worked with a few film crews myself, I know that would have been no easy task to achieve.

***

One of the questions most world-weary people ask me when we discuss reincarnation is: 'Do I have to reincarnate; can't I just opt to stay in the afterlife?'

Turning to the world of spirit I asked John Dingwall whether, given the current state of the world, there is a lot of apprehension by souls preparing for their next lifetime. As he so often has in past connections John provided a very appropriate example, with the input of his spirit team.

'Barry, I want you to imagine that we are floating away in the spirit world. I'm your guide and I'm about to send you into another life on Earth. You would be terrified, because you know how much temptation is there and how so much can go wrong in your next life.' John went on to say that I would know that spirit is not sending me into a lovely divine landscape, but into a confusing and unstable time. Being in the peaceful atmosphere of the world of spirit, this would be very concerning as I contemplated the future being laid out in front of me.

When I pointed out that surely history is full of uncertain times — wars, pestilence, brutality, poverty, starvation and so on — John said we are now going through a period of global turbulence like no other in recorded history. That set me back on my heels, despite the fact I was sitting down at the time.

This raised the question of life choices. If a soul had the opportunity, wouldn't it opt for a protected and comfortable lifestyle in peaceful surroundings and not a life full of challenges?

'A soul who genuinely wanted to better their advancement would immediately go into a poorer life, because we [in the world of spirit] all know there are better lessons to be learned in those circumstances. There's also a greater capacity there to make a difference for the right person, such as the Mother Theresas of the world.' John explained further that a very challenging life lived in poverty and with great trials is often followed by a more comfortable future lifetime. (That sounded a bit like the carrot and the stick philosophy to me, I must admit.) It all comes down to how we conduct each life, how we cope with various experiences and, most importantly, what we learn. Even in a lifetime in which we have a lot of money and material wealth, we can still do much to help people. Our choices and actions determine our soul development, not the trappings of life, no matter in what circumstances we find ourselves. For me, this really underlines the whole philosophy and raison d'être of reincarnation.

John went on to say he is not particularly looking forward to coming back for his next life as he is very happy to be in the spirit world. The question is: does he get a choice; can he refuse to come back?

'Not really,' he said, with a resigned laugh. We can often negotiate around the life we are coming back to but, as John says, 'who is to say my choices are the right ones? They may not be for my highest good.'

The whole question of a suitable life is not just an individual one; it may involve guides, elders and even a large group of souls providing their input in a concentrated meditation communication.

I then tossed in a question about the story of our birth in each lifetime: is it just a random event? The answer I was given is that the time, date and place of our birth is part of the life package we embrace and, yes, astrology is not only valid in the eyes of spirit but is an essential element of each person's new life. There are no accidents, no surprises and no mistakes around our time of birth — we are on a predestined path for our succession of lifetimes — and although many people equate astrology with a couple of lines in a newspaper column, our astrology chart is actually our lives' blueprint.

John was adamant that most people don't realise how significant the time of birth is for everyone. 'It's an important part of the spirit world and our individual spiritual development, and the timing for each individual spirit being placed in their next life [on Earth] is of the utmost importance.'

The timing of each incarnation is extremely important not only for that spirit, but in the context of other important relationships during their lifetime. Our astrology chart not only outlines our strengths, abilities and challenges, but also helps set and control those aspects of our life that are pre-ordained. Our lives contain a number of destiny points and karmic influences, which then allow us to employ free will to make choices that affect that particular lifetime, and often future lives as well.

It is an individual thing as to when our cycle of reincarnation ends; there is no general rule of thumb, no set number of lives to be lived. We are each on a unique spiritual quest. Even if our life cycle on Earth may have reached its end point, there are still many other worlds and dimensions for us to experience. In fact, many people have a history of lives on Earth as well as other worlds (this is explained further in Chapter 22). This especially applies to the young generation of children coming onto the planet now. Many of them are bringing accumulated wisdom and experience from numerous different worlds, dimensions and even universes to help our world as it experiences many changes.

Chapter 10

EXPLORING PAST LIVES WHILE IN THE AFTERLIFE

We tend to think that uncovering our past lives is a therapy that we only pursue while we are in our earthly incarnation to find answers to current problems and situations.

Nothing could be further from the truth.

Essentially, our current state of being represents the accumulation of every past thought and experience we have had from the time we broke away from source to become an independent soul energy. Not only do the experiences we have in each lifetime contribute to this state, but they also influence our activities during our life-between-lives development. An integral part of our soul energy is created and developed while we are in the afterlife. We may be resting and recovering during this time, but our learning continues.

While communicating with John and his spirit team, I learned that our guides allow us to revisit our past lives when they deem it appropriate as part of the ongoing evolution of our soul. At what stage this happens after we return to the afterlife depends on the individual concerned. After a long and complicated passing the soul may need a lot of healing before the next stage of development happens, which would include past-life research. For others, investigating the past could begin virtually straightaway and even be part of the healing process.

We don't have unrestricted access to research into past lives as we would in a library; we have to have the permission and direction of guides or elders or sometimes a higher, more evolved spirit connected with a previous life. The best-known way to access past-life information is often through the Hall of Records or the Akashic Records, which contains universal records from time immemorial of every lifetime, thought, word and intent. Information outside our own personal lives is only available to those granted special permission. Our guides decide which aspect of our past and sometimes our future lives is considered appropriate to our development during the life-between-lives sojourn.

As there is no physical body, the contact is established with each soul telepathically like a kind of meditation and when we are in a quiet state and open to receive it. All communication in the world of spirit is done through thought. There would seem to be a parallel with the regression techniques we use on Earth, but without the physical body getting in the way. Knowledge is shared in many different ways according to the level the soul had reached. It uses all the senses, ranging from what we would describe as a dream — including taste, smell and sound — through to holographic images. It also relies on the person's willingness to face the truth even when harsh realities are revealed.

When John mentioned spirits sitting quietly with their eyes closed to receive telepathic communication it surprised me, as I thought surely they have no eyes to close. John said many spirits still feel the need to have a connection with their human form and will create the sensation of eyes and ears and the ability of speech. This is just another example of the flexibility of life in the world of spirit.

I couldn't resist the temptation to ask John whether he had visited his past lives since returning to the afterlife. He told me about a significant life he led as a very poor woman living in mediaeval times. 'That life taught me a hell of a lot: humility, suffering, disease and famine. It taught me more than anything else about the love of children that were taken away from me in that life. It was a life of loss.'

So why did he need to review that life?

'We easily forget the lessons that are taught to us. A lot of lessons learned in human form will have to be taught over and over again.' He explained further how amazingly easy it is for us to let go of that information and allow our minds to be clouded. We are often our own worst enemy as we let our minds fool us into not believing the information we are given. We know deep in our hearts the right course of action, but the mind can play tricks to help us justify ignoring what is best for us. These lessons keep intensifying through various incarnations until we are forced to take notice.

Sometimes it would appear the only way we can best learn our lesson and move on is by clearing the past obstacles our soul has brought into this life.

Chapter 11

JACK'S LIFE IN THE CIVIL WAR

Time passes quickly on Earth, especially around Christmas as one year ends and another begins, and it was four months after my past-life sessions with Peter Smith that I listened to the recording of my second regression. After revisiting a lifetime in ancient Greece in our first session, I was curious to know where to next as Pete took me into very a deep hypnotic state, even deeper than that previously reached.

To be honest, I could not initially recall the details of this second regression as I started to listen to the recording of this excursion into my past. However, after a few minutes my memory banks clicked into place and I vaguely remembered revisiting my life as an English army officer who became embroiled in the American Civil War in the 1860s.

This lifetime came as no great surprise as my late friend Bob Murray, a wonderful medium and author who lived in Canada, had in 2012 sent me the transcript of a life we shared in those turbulent times; I included this episode in my book *No Goodbyes*. Having always known deep down that I fought in the American Civil War, I was happy that Bob's investigations answered any questions I may have had about those times.

Bob was a frequent guest on my radio program *RadioOutThere* before he passed in 2015. He had brought me many valued messages from spirit over the years and we formed a close friendship even though we lived in different parts of the world. We never got to meet in the flesh this time around, but both felt intuitively that we had strong past-life connections.

As the story unfolded under Peter's guidance I wondered why my subconscious had taken me back to this life again: surely I already had all the answers to my original questions? However, safe in the knowledge that spirit obviously had more to share about this lifetime. I settled back to listen to the recording ...

Deep in trance, as my vision cleared I saw that it was dusk and I was holding a flaming torch while waiting quietly on a clifftop overlooking the ocean. It was around 1864 and I described my appearance as being 'about 30 years of age, wearing light-coloured pants tucked into riding boots fitted with spurs, a white shirt with a ribbon tie and a dark jacket'. I was wearing a broad-brimmed hat and had the appearance of a gentleman; I was 'certainly not of the working class'. The new moon gave sufficient light for me to spy a wagon approaching from the coast loaded with boxes of guns and ammunition, which was being delivered to my colleague and myself.

When Peter asked me to describe my circumstances it emerged that I was one of two English army officers sent by the government to remain neutral but to bring in all sorts of supplies to help the Confederate army. We also had to set up lines of communication between the South and the government in London. When questioned about why the English government would want to help the South, I answered that it was because of an agreement made before the war began.

My friend and fellow officer William had arrived with me in Carolina with enough money for us to establish our identity as gentlemen traders representing English companies still eager for cotton and other crops from the South. When we arrived trade was still being carried on in Charleston, despite the blockade by Union naval forces. We never disclosed the fact to anyone that we were English army officers.

(Historical records show that the English government was keeping open the option of recognising the Confederate government in the early years of the war. It makes sense that they would need to keep abreast of the fluctuating conditions of the conflict, so William and I were basically working as secret agents.)

When asked to give some personal details about myself in this life, I replied that I was the youngest son of an English nobleman who fought in the Napoleonic War. This meant my older brother would inherit the entire estate and it was expected of me that I would go into the army. I served in India in the late 1850s at the time of the infamous Indian Mutiny, after which I returned to London with the rank of captain. My army experience covered many different activities over the years and I apparently earned the nickname of 'Jack' (of all trades?).

At this point in the regression Jack was asked to provide more intricate details of the mission.

Jack's colleague William was a major at the time they were sent to America, attached to the Royal Engineers and based at Aldershot. They first met in India when they were both serving there in the late 1850s and became firm friends. When given his mission, William told his superiors he wanted Jack to work with him in America and so a partnership was formed.

When the Civil War broke out in America people in England were anxious for news, as they were not sure how events half a world away would affect their lives. Trade was the first area hit, especially with such important crops as tobacco and cotton being restricted. As the war progressed, news from America was a highly debated issue in Britain.

The two officers were ordered to travel to what Jack simply described as Carolina — most likely Charleston in South Carolina, where English blockade runners were still able to bring in small shipments of supplies for the South. On their arrival they were to connect with a Major O'Donohue to work out how they could arrange for goods to come and go between England and the South.

Peter's voice then took Jack back to the new moon clifftop meeting.

He and William successfully took delivery of the smuggled arms and rode west, where they eventually met up with a squad of Confederate soldiers to hand over the goods. This was apparently the first delivery of what was to become a fairly typical transaction for the two officers. Blockade runners employed smaller types of vessels able to outrun the Union naval ships, but were only able to bring in small shipments at a time.

Jack and William had established themselves in Charleston where, as Jack put it, 'we had digs at the hotel'. They had money to spend and 'young ladies to entertain them and a lot of whisky to be drunk' as they carefully established their new image.

'We needed to create the right appearance, and above all we were not to let them know we were English soldiers. There are still many who hate the English, even after all this time.' The Confederate army was desperate to smuggle in as many arms and general supplies as possible and blockade runners were essential to their survival in the war.

Peter took Jack forward to the next significant part of their mission. Jack's immediate reaction was 'the Yankees are coming!' He associated the invading Union forces with the town of Yorktown, which had seen a decisive battle fought in 1862 following a siege, after which a Union army military garrison was established there. In 1864, the year Jack and William were in America, the army abandoned the garrison as Union forces attacked the Confederate rebels.

Jack and William travelled north to Virginia on the orders of General Lee, who unsurprisingly knew about them and their mission all along. By now the rebel army was falling apart and, in Jack's words, 'It's becoming more of a struggle for them … there have been desertions and a lot of trouble … they were getting very rag-tag now, and we were told the Yankees are winning the war.' Lee ordered his soldiers to stop and dig in to prepare to meet the enemy. Jack recounted a meeting he had with the general at his headquarters at what Jack described as a mansion (Beasley House,

Petersburg). 'He looked tired,' was all Jack had to say about the meeting.

Lee said he was commissioning them into the Confederate army, much against the wishes of Jack. The general needed their military expertise and discipline as his position was becoming desperate. 'I had a sense of foreboding. We were not there to fight; we were there to trade, to help and to represent our government. In our military we do things differently.' Lee told Jack their escape route was now shut off. There were no more ships getting through the blockade, so they were stranded.

Jack revealed he and William had also run out of money, so there was no choice but to reluctantly accept General Lee's commission. 'I can sympathise, but it's not my fight,' Jack said. He was also upset that he had to leave behind a woman he had been with in Charleston, who as he was leaving discovered she was pregnant with his child.

At that point Jack saw fires in the distance and realised that the Union troops were setting fire to plantations as they prepared to attack. 'The damn Yankees are coming. There's a lot of panic in the town and women and children are being evacuated in the face of the imminent danger. Jack began to suspect that Lee had always intended to draft them into his army because of their combined military skills and experience.

[Historical note: the siege of Petersburg, some 35 kilometres south from the capitol Richmond, began in 1864 and lasted for nine months. The two cities were ringed by Union troops, which meant the Confederate forces were slowly being strangled. The siege culminated in the famous Battle of Petersburg from June 1864 to March 1865, after which General Robert E. Lee surrendered. The war finished shortly after that.]

Jack and William were sent north towards Richmond where the Northern army was threatening to overwhelm Lee's forces, which were spread thinly to protect the rail link, and ordered to build a defensive redoubt. This was where William's engineering skills were undoubtedly called into play. Jack had gained some artillery experience in India and helped the Confederates position their cannon. Lee had assured them they were to be mainly used in an advisory capacity, but Jack said they were also 'involved in the fray' from time to time.

The two Englishmen were issued with rifles for their own protection; however, Jack said while he was happy to advise he did not want to kill. 'It's not like shooting Indians, mutineers or thieves and rogues when we were in India. They'd steal anything over there … poor beggars were starving in many cases. That didn't give them the right to steal, so sometimes we had to shoot them, to teach them [the others] a lesson.'

Jack reveals there is a battle about to happen and he is feeling tense, his voice now barely above a whisper. 'It's early light … first thing in the morning. We have their front line covered with our artillery … We are stretched; they outnumber us. I wonder whether I will see England again.'

Peter asked Jack what had happened to him. 'They're attacking. Oh my God, they've come up on our flank, we've been outflanked! Where are our scouts; why didn't they tell us? We are vastly outnumbered … their artillery is now pounding us too. They are coming at us.' Jack is reliving the experience as the battle swirls around him.

Jack's voice is reduced to a whisper: 'I've been shot … in the chest. It's getting dark, getting dark.'

Jack's voice fades off into silence.

***

Revisiting past lives is not merely some Hollywood time-tunnel experience; there has to be a valid reason for it to be meaningful. So what were the lessons and messages that emerged from connecting with Jack a century and a half ago?

As Jack slips into the surrounding darkness, Peter Smith asks whether this was his moment to be set free or if there was something else he had to do after being shot in the chest.

'I seem to be in a dark tunnel, but … there's light coming out. It's very light.' Jack's voice takes on a new strength and he exclaims: 'My God, there's an angel. I didn't think they really existed. We always joked about angels: were they real, or did we make them up? Oh, there's a smaller one as well.' Jack gives a long sigh, 'Aaahh, I guess I must be dead!'

Peter tells Jack's spirit to let go and expand into its full consciousness in this beautiful state of being. Jack's voice takes on a disconnected tone of floating freely: 'There's clouds boiling all around me; clouds, mist, it's almost as if they're bearing me up. There's somebody coming towards me … it's my father! I didn't know he was dead He must have died while I was in America.'

Peter asks how Jack's father greets him. Jack's voice sounds a little surprised: 'He welcomes me, "*Welcome home, my son*," he says. This is home? I thought home was in England.'

Now safely back home in the afterlife, Jack describes his state of being as 'floating, I'm just floating. It's all very peaceful.'

Peter then asks Jack's spirit, 'How do we get a sense of the purpose behind Jack's life?' The reply was interesting: 'I've been told it was another life as a soldier ... expectations ... I didn't want to be a soldier, it was expected of me.' Jack's voice sounds wistful as he looks back on the life he has just left: 'It was expected of me. I was the younger son, I had no choice. My father's estate went to my brother Hugo.'

Peter asks Jack what he learned from that life.

Jack says he realised war is always a waste of life and we need to be able to find ways to do more than kill other people, otherwise 'we just become another spoke in the wheel'. Looking back on his life, Jack describes it as a good life in many ways but he senses he could have done a lot more. 'I was only young when I died ... thirty-six ... never married.' Jack regrets the situation around the girl he left behind. When prompted, Jack remembers 'the name she called herself by was Fanny', describing her as a fun girl. When asked whether she is someone in Barry's life today he replies: 'It was someone who Barry had a brief association with.' (My guide later confirmed that it was my partner Judy, who passed in 1997 after we had been together for four years. Judy's story is told in depth in my previous books, but suffice to say she is the one who inspired my writing about the afterlife.)

When asked what happened to Fanny, all Jack would say was that Fanny lost the child of his she was carrying.

Peter then connected via Jack with my soul energy and asked to access all the lifetimes he had in the military to find out what he needs to learn in this lifetime. Deep in hypnotic trance, my soul replied that I had many lives in the military. 'Some were by choice. I needed to learn about the taking of life, the attitude of the cheapness of life, not respecting life. Life was cheap; it was just *other people's lives*. If they were getting in the way for whatever reason, take their life.'

When asked if this lesson has been learned now my soul replied: 'Oh, yes, no more warrior lives; it ended on the Somme. The futility, the degradation, the horror, the senselessness, the terror, fear, hatred … all part of something that is so destructive … and so useless.'

My immediate past life was as Brian, a 19-year-old British soldier in the muddy trenches of France, who died on 1 July 1916 on the first day of the infamous Battle of the Somme. I have written about this life in detail in my book *Afterlife: Uncovering the Secrets of Life After Death.*

Peter asked my soul energy by what name I was known in the place from which I was currently communicating. The reply was rather elusive at first: 'I don't really have a name, I'm just accepted.' Peter probed a little further, asking how I wished him to address me. 'Any way you choose; I'll know it is me you are speaking to. You can call me Jack, or call me Brian, feel free.'

Peter kept probing to get deeper into my essence as a spirit, asking when he addressed me if it would be in his knowing of me beyond Jack or Brian, or even Barry. His patience paid off. 'I have a spiritual name that is very long and complicated. It starts with V, so perhaps you can call me V.'

Peter asked V to look across the spectrum of his lives to ascertain what Barry needs to know at this point of his life. V immediately replied: 'Loyalty, understanding, the need for humanity, the union of souls and peace ... the hardest of all things. The key is love.' V made a reference to a biblical saying that describes 'a peace that surpasses all understanding'.

Peter asked V why Barry chose this life to express his soul purpose, what the main influence was. 'Communication,' was V's immediate response. 'Barry was always meant to communicate information, to communicate in many different ways and modalities for different effects.'

Peter then asked V about the deeper purpose behind this book about past lives.

'The correlation of past lives. The word journey is much used on Earth, too much ... The progression of souls, the lessons, the ability to make mistakes and learn, the ability to accept others for who they are ... Those are harsh lessons to learn.'

When asked what he wanted Barry to know, V replied: 'He is protected, he is guided and he still has work to do. This is a significant life, with many opportunities for his own growth and for helping others.'

And for the readers of this book, what is the overall theme they can take away with them? 'This is just one of many lives ... the past is who we are.'

***

Looking back on the details of such an intense past-life regression as this can open many doors of understanding. There are of course questions that pop into the mind of even a true believer such as myself, such as are all these details for real or is my imagination making some of this up? Then something happens to dispel these doubts, some confirmation arises, and that is certainly the case with this chapter of my life.

Peter addressed V, my soul energy, while I was in deep trance, mentioning that earlier he had set up a corridor in my subconscious that addressed the lineage of my soul to allow me to step through doors and tell stories to help in my research for this book. He asked if there was anything in my lineage that needed to be added that would make it easier for my soul to express.

The answer was instant and to the point: 'No, just tell him to go through the green door. He knows ... there will be new knowledge, insights ... no two visits will ever be the same.'

It was only four months later as I listened to these words on the recording of the session for the first time that I heard the reference to the green door. At first I was puzzled, but then a sudden realisation hit me and I knew what my soul was referring to. Many years ago I had been given a set of Tarot cards that I only ever occasionally used for telephone readings. An image of a card featuring a green door materialised in my mind and I reached for the cards to confirm my vision. I soon found the card, which showed a large stone archway surrounding the aforesaid green door with a golden-coloured ring with which to open it. My eyes flicked to the message at the top of the card, and I almost fell off my seat. It read *Endings and Beginnings* – which for me denotes transformation and past lives.

When I rang Peter Smith to tell him what I had discovered he was as shocked and delighted as I was. We both believe that far from being dismissed as some form of coincidence, this was indeed a confirmation from my soul energy that I was on the right path.

Peter also asked V if there was anything else to share with Barry. The answer was: 'Look after his heart; there is a feeling of stress around the heart.' Is this physical, spiritual or emotional? 'Yes, all three.' (In 2009 I was diagnosed with atrial fibrillation, or an irregular heart beat.)

Peter asked what could be done to help Barry. 'He must help himself.' What do you recommend? 'Tolerance, understanding, empathy … Love, that's very important.'

Peter then asked V if there was anything more to say before he brought Barry out of trance.

'No, this is enough for the time being. Love has been sent from spirit, and from his higher self and from those in spirit who love, help and support him. They are with him when he needs them, and sometimes when he doesn't.'

To hear such a warm and loving message from my soul energy made me tingle all over. At that point we reached the end of the session, and Peter instructed me to come back into my body and to this reality. My voice grumbled in reply like a small child: 'Don't want to.'

An interesting footnote to the reminiscences of my life in the Civil

War came in the guise of a message from nature. Our indigenous peoples on this planet all accept that we humans are part of the greater picture, which includes birds, animals and all aspects of nature, a principle with which I heartily agree.

As I started to listen to the recording of the life of Jack, a finely plumed young currawong, a native Australian mostly black bird with bright yellow eyes, perched itself on the railing of the deck adjoining my office. It called out in a strong, demanding voice that immediately drew my attention. The currawong now comes every day as I write, calling out the same message, and makes strong eye contact with me before flying away into the trees.

When I checked *Animal Dreaming, The Symbolic and Spiritual Language of the Australian Animals* by Scott Alexander King (Rockpool Publishing, 2003), I saw the following message:

> Currawong – Ghost Wisdom. Currawong Dreaming helps weed out the rubbish from our past, to cut out the spiritual deadwood and to cull the weaker sides of our personality. It helps us to face our inner demons and overcome them. Ghost Wisdom deals with negative aspects from our past that continue to haunt us. It provides a means to heal them and to view them as facets of future Dreaming. Tools created from experience that we can offer to others as stepping stones to their own healing.

For me, that says it all.

Chapter 12

PAST LIVES AS FAMOUS PEOPLE

One of the biggest problems many people have in accepting the principle of past lives is their scepticism about those who claim to have been someone famous in a past life. The number of people who claim to have previously lived as Cleopatra is often thrown up for scorn when past lives are discussed.

I am in agreement. That so many famous people from the past are apparently now living quiet lives in the suburbs of Australia and various other countries of the world is something that does not sit well with my investigations. When I raised the question with Peter Ramster, who has conducted many hundreds of regressions, he confirmed he has never come across anyone who was even slightly famous, let alone a historical figure of note. Other regression experts such as Peter Smith, who took me back into my past for the purposes of writing this book, have found the same thing.

So what happens to famous people when they pass on: do they come back as lesser mortals or what? Who better to ask than John Dingwall, my spokespirit for the team that has all the answers to questions of this nature?

John explained that most people's claims of past fame are

simply wishful thinking, that it is nothing more than an exercise in ego and a matter of power and control with some individuals. However, he added that many famous people who are now in spirit are indeed making contact with people on Earth in what we refer to as channelling sessions. 'The reason they are making contact is the same as we are doing now: trying to better the world by getting a message out. A lot of them were very good at communicating [in that past life] so communicating the [same] way we are now is second nature.'

Persisting with my line of thought, I asked John about those who had attained very high positions of power in the past. Where are they now? He confirmed that while each story is unique, some spirits do keep coming back to Earth with even higher positions of power and influence than they previously enjoyed because they have missions to carry out. Many of these spirits may never access their past during their current incarnation, as this could be very confusing for all concerned. Quite understandably, I couldn't draw him out with any names.

Another piece of the famous person puzzle is that there are also mischievous spirits who are pretending to be someone famous just to create confusion. It seems this is a question with no simple answer that explains everything.

On another tack, I enquired about the possibility of the existence of an *aspect* of a person now on Earth that is part of a previous life. 'You may bring in to physical life aspects of several previous lives all at once, even if you don't realise it. You are bringing the experience of all those lives, and they are all hopefully gelling together to advance you spiritually.'

In other words, a soul's earthly experiences are a progression, and at any point along the way represent the sum total of all previous existences. This would explain John's point about why famous people usually keep advancing in their soul progression unless they really fall off the perch in a big way.

'This idea that you could be a king in one life and an inmate of a refugee camp in the next could happen, but it's not necessarily so.' However, he went on to talk about the free will in each lifetime that can completely alter the events that were pre-ordained for that person. He likened our soul's path to that of the trunk of a tree: it grows solidly in one direction, but there are branches that grow in various sizes and directions along the way. Each tree has its own unique growth pattern.

My guides and advisers in the world of spirit have many ways of getting messages to me, as evidenced in my visitor in the night in Chapter 4. While I was writing this chapter I received an email from one of the listeners to my program *RadioOutThere* reminding me of an interview I had done many years ago with US author and medium Sharon Prince. Sharon is also a qualified psychologist with an MEd in science education, and my listener recalled a fascinating interview we had involving past lives. When the penny eventually dropped, I remembered this was my instance of contact with a world-famous figure from long ago; the full story is in Chapter 13.

What about the famous religious figures from ancient times: Jesus, Buddha and ascended masters, for example? Do they ever reincarnate after their very special lifetime? 'Generally their energy is spread around in spirit, so everybody gets a small piece of it and it's put to good use. Their future is better served being in the spirit world; they can do higher good from here.' Part of their energy will be incorporated into the body and soul of a person who is destined to have a very positive impact on their time in history.

Chapter 13

THE MAN WHO WALKED WITH JESUS

Despite people's claims of having been a famous historical figure, I have only come across one genuine case study in my research.

Imagine having some 18 psychics and mediums walking up to you in public places and announcing that you walked with Jesus 2,000 years ago? This is what actually happened to John Davis, a professional comedian and mediaeval fight performer at Renaissance festivals in the US and Canada.

John Davis' story has been recounted by Sharon Prince in her book *John of Old, John of New.* I interviewed Sharon in 2006, and had forgotten about this intriguing story until one of the listeners to my radio program *RadioOutThere* contacted me in 2017 and jogged my memory. I was in the middle of writing this book at the time, and I am convinced this was not a coincidence but another example of how my contacts in the spirit world are helping me write *Past Lives Unveiled.*

Reading John's amazing story again after all those years was very stirring, as I had lost touch with both him and Sharon. Sharon recalled first meeting him while she was doing intuitive readings on the 'Renaissance circuit', as she described it. These are festivals where actors dress up and recreate events and fight scenes, as well as enjoy food and entertainment, from around the time of King Henry VIII.

Sharon met John Davis when they were staying at the house of a mutual friend in Ontario in Canada while on tour. They were in a room full of people and John was sitting in a corner; as Sharon said: 'He was not so much looking at them, but looking around them.' When John looked up and focused on her she realised he was looking at her aura. So Sharon walked straight up to him and said, 'I know what you're doing; you're looking at my aura, aren't you?'

Sharon described his reaction as being like a kid with his hand caught in the cookie jar. She further shocked John when she told him he was a healer, something he'd been told before but had not followed up. He did admit to Sharon he'd had out-of-body experiences and the sensation of Kundalini rising, which is acknowledged as a spiritual awakening. He also told her about seeing an angel and having a past-life experience.

Sharon told John that she was doing intuitive readings on the tour, and over the next couple of weeks he sent several people to see her. She later discovered he was checking her out as he was a sceptic about readings. The feedback was positive, and John eventually relented and came to her for a reading at the next stage of the tour in Maryland.

Sharon looked back on the reading, which was about John's personal life, and he was amazed at her accuracy. However, as she was wrapping up her guides told her something astonishing, which she blurted out without thinking: 'I'm being told you walked with Jesus.'

John was just as astounded as Sharon at this piece of information but his immediate reply was 'Yes, I did', because deep down he realised it was true. John then arranged for another reading with Sharon to gain more information. Sharon agreed, laughingly telling him not to freak out if they found he was an apostle!

A few weeks later they sat in the sand dunes above a beach to do the reading, and Sharon immediately felt a very strong surge of energy surround her. Despite not being a religious person she recognised the presence of Jesus, or 'Jeshua' as she referred to him. She was overwhelmed with emotion by the energy, but John remained solid and supportive as she passed on Jeshua's message.

John later told her that her spine then straightened up as she sat slumped on the sand, her face became completely calm with a look of bliss and suddenly all her trepidation melted away. Jeshua then spoke: 'John of old, John of new, I love you, I have always loved you, I will always love you, I was with you, I will always be with you.' He went on to tell John that he had chosen John for this mission and had come to pave the way for him.

When I asked Sharon whether she felt like she was making this up, she replied that she didn't feel that way at all as the energy was 'so present and so strong it was just working through me'. Sharon described a feeling of both John and herself being embraced by unconditional love and incredible energy that still remained indescribable. Jeshua went on to reveal that John will see him in the body he possessed in Galilee in this lifetime.

Jeshua then asked John whether he would like to see him and when John replied that he would, Jeshua told him to close his eyes. At first John didn't see anything, but when he was told to focus he found himself as Sharon described: in full sensory awareness, his face in the sand covered by his hands. When John raised his head the sand fell away from his face and he saw a sandal in front of his eyes. Raising his head, John saw the face of Jesus with a back light surrounding it. The light then faded and John found himself back on the beach, feeling still dazed and a little confused by his vision.

A few months later John did a meditation where he was taken to a past life in which he was walking along a beach in Galilee. He realised the vision he had was 'after Jesus had died and was resurrected', and he was so shocked he fell face first into the sand.

Sharon recalls intuitively knowing that the events on the beach were genuine, and from then on both their lives were changed forever.

Later that afternoon Sharon took a walk down to the beach on her own to gather her thoughts on what had happened that day. John later confided that he saw 'a plume of light that came out of her crown chakra and wound its way into the sky'. John later joked that it looked like an umbilical cord to God!

Later in the interview on *RadioOutThere*, Sharon related a fascinating event that happened to John in the time between his two readings with Sharon. John was on stage for his live show, and he locked eyes with a man in the audience in his early 30s with long brown hair and a beard who looked remarkably like Jesus. It was a stiflingly hot day and the audience was feeling the heat badly, but this young man, dressed in a long-sleeved white shirt and jeans, did not show any evidence of the heat.

John kept being drawn back to this man, who had fixed his gaze on John, and their eyes locked on several occasions. As the act drew to a close and the audience stood up to leave, John looked over again but the man had disappeared. When he told Sharon the story during their second reading they both felt it was definitely a manifestation.

Sharon didn't cross paths with John Davis for about a year, and had come to the conclusion that her apostolic adventure had run its course. Returning from a trip to Scotland, Sharon found a voicemail message from John telling her she had to get hold of a book co-authored by Edgar Cayce called *Edgar Cayce on the Millennium: The Famed Prophet Visualizes a Bright New World*. John excitedly told Sharon of a passage he had discovered in the book that stated that 'John the Beloved would reincarnate before the millennium and that his name would again be John'.

Sharon started shaking with reaction to this news, and thought to herself that maybe all this was real after all and she wasn't going crazy. It took a couple of days for her head to stop spinning before she resolved to follow through with this new revelation. She rationalised that if she could channel Jeshua for John, then why not see if she could connect with him for herself? Still feeling troubled, Sharon went for a walk in the fields behind her house and put out the request for confirmation that John Davis is in fact the reincarnation of John the Beloved.

Sharon experienced an almost immediate surge of energy,

followed by the feeling of a hand on her left temple. She later felt that it was a way for her to focus her consciousness so that she knew it was indeed the spirit of Jeshua communicating with her. Sharon heard the words clearly in her mind: 'What do you think?' She thought the energy was so strong that it wasn't her mind playing tricks on her. Sharon replied: 'I don't know; that's why I'm asking you.' Jeshua then asked, 'What is your heart telling you?' Sharon was a little nonplussed, but Jeshua went on: 'Listen to your heart, for it will always tell you the truth. You are part of an angelic presence known as the Sacred Heart.' When Sharon asked what that was, he told her to 'look it up'. Sharon realised that Jeshua does have a good sense of humour.

Sharon asked why she was the one chosen to work with John Davis, helping him to discover his past. Jeshua told her that she and John had worked together in a past life and it was decided before she was born that she would work with him again.

Sharon also discovered that despite being the physical reincarnation of the apostle, John Davis wasn't the only person on the planet embracing John the Beloved's soul energy. There are several others around the world who have brought back part of John the Beloved's energy into this life. As she continued her work, Sharon has also discovered what she referred to as the phenomenon of several women she knows who have memories of being Mary Magdalene. The message these women are spreading is so important and so prodigious that it could not possibly be imparted by just one person.

I have always believed that the fragmentation of soul energy is one rational explanation for those people who, under hypnotic regression, identify with the life of some historical figure or other celebrity — although there could be many reasons over and above bringing the universal message of the soul energy with which they identify. For many people it could just be tuning into the universal consciousness so they can work on and resolve issues or karma from past lives.

Sharon mentioned she had discovered that the soul of the apostle John had split into three energies to help spread the word of the importance of love in our lives, which was the essential message of Jesus over 2,000 years ago. The message John and Sharon received today comes more from Jeshua as an ascended master or enlightened being than some sort of religious connection.

An interesting addition to this story is Sharon Prince's own past-life association. When I interviewed her on radio in 2017 she was reluctant at first to discuss this, describing herself as being shy about it. Like so many of us, Sharon has doubted those people who claim to have been a famous figure in history. When I pushed her, she gave in and told her story.

Raised as a strict Mormon in the 1960s and 1970s, Sharon remembers her father showing her a Time Life book called *The Tower of London*. She recalls that the illustrations in the book caught her young eye, and in her words: 'I opened up to a page and there was this woman in a Tudor dress, and I looked down and saw the name Lady Jane Grey.' Sharon then had an unexpected reaction: 'Out of my mouth before I even knew what I was saying I cried, that's me!' She remembers thinking, 'What did I just say?'

There was nothing in her family background or education that would cause such a reaction. Like all her school mates, she had only studied American history and knew little about English history. She had heard about Henry VIII and his wives, but knew nothing else about those times. The first time Sharon was even exposed to the idea of past lives was many years later when she read about it in Shirley MacLaine's books.

When Sharon went to England for the first time years later in 1990 she went on a guided tour. 'I remember going to the Tower of London, and that was a heady kind of experience.' She also visited Warwick Castle in Warwickshire, and when she went into the great hall she felt very uneasy. Her husband couldn't understand her reaction and thought she was crazy when she blurted out: 'I've been here before.' She then became fixated on the giant fireplace in the hall, and could not take her eyes off it for some strange reason.

The following year, by then back in the US, Sharon started developing her metaphysical skills and visited a past-life regressionist in Texas. The hypnotist took her back to this lifetime in Tudor England to try and find the answers to some of the questions that were troubling her.

'It started out very slowly,' Sharon recalls. 'It was as if I was in a movie; I was feeling the coldness of the room I was standing in. I had bare feet and was wearing a simple, greyish [-coloured] kind of dress, a drab kind of dress. I was standing with my father and there was a bunch of windows behind him; it was a kind of hallway. He was talking about my high purpose in life, something that I'm meant to do.'

Sharon was then taken into another memory where she was getting married, and had started to cry at that point in the ceremony. She described this as being really weird, because she was not being wed at the altar but was standing to the right of it. Standing next to her was a man dressed in red and gold, who she described as being very handsome. When asked why she was crying she replied, 'Because I don't love this man and I'm being forced to marry him against my will.'

A few years later Sharon discovered a book written by UK writer Leanda de Lisle entitled *The Sisters Who Would Be Queen*, which told how Lady Jane Grey was married off by Lord Dudley to his son to manipulate the succession to the throne. It was part of a two-way marriage with one of Lady Jane's sisters to the Earl of Pembroke's heir, all occurring during the same ceremony.

Thinking in 2017 about her regression, Sharon's recalled a series of events she was later able to verify when she did her research. She remembers a man who made her laugh a lot who she called Uncle Tom. Later research indicated that this was in fact Thomas Seymour, who had married the Dowager Queen Catherine Parr after the death of Henry VIII. Lady Jane had gone to live with Catherine Parr. Sharon recalls feeling closer to Catherine Parr than she did to her own mother, and describes her as 'being sweet and loving to all the children there'. At that time the young Princess Elizabeth, later Queen Elizabeth I, was one of those children in the household. History also shows that Lady Jane was sold as a ward to Seymour for £2000 to arrange a future marriage, once again in the manipulation for succession to the throne.

When Edward VI died Jane Grey was hastily made queen, although she had no real authority as Lord Dudley was the power behind the throne. Jane Grey's reign lasted only nine days before an uprising saw Princess Mary take her place; Jane was sent to the Tower of London. She was held in the tower for many months before Mary was persuaded, albeit reluctantly, to have her executed.

Sharon's regression took her to the time of her execution. She said Lady Jane felt betrayed, that she had never asked to be queen and none of it was fair. 'I remember looking up before being blindfolded and seeing a huge tree over the scaffold. It must have been a very beautiful day as the sky was very blue behind it. I remember it as the last thing she ever saw before being blindfolded.' The beheading itself was not the horrible thing we probably all imagine. Jane felt no pain when the axe fell, but rather a sensation that 'I am no longer able to sustain life any more. It felt so weird. I was still conscious in my head, but I was aware my body was no longer attached to it.' Jane then felt herself lifting up out of the body and moving away from Earth. At this stage the regressionist brought Sharon back to the present day.

Sharon later told me the main issue that emerged for her from recalling this lifetime was trust. She has identified several members of her current family she associates with people from the life she lived as Lady Jane. Her father in this life was the father in that life too. She remembers standing in front of the fireplace at Warwick Castle while her then father discussed her future with two other men. She remembers feeling that as her fate was being decided it was as if she wasn't even there in the room. Such was the situation for women in those days — they were basically regarded as chattels.

Sharon recognised her now ex-husband as being her executioner in that lifetime. On one occasion they were shopping in J.C. Penney's department store and he started touching the back of her neck. She described this as being an unusual movement and a part of her she hated him touching. She told him a couple of times to stop before loudly exclaiming: 'Take your hands off my neck!' This was before she knew about his role in her past life, but later it all made sense when she did her research into Lady Jane's life.

When visiting the Tower of London sometime later, Sharon just 'knew' where Lady Jane was buried even though it wasn't marked; a Beefeater confirmed this for her. She felt nauseous when standing where the scaffold on which Lady Jane had been beheaded stood even though the spot wasn't marked out. She couldn't explain her feeling of nausea at the time, but it all became clear when she later discovered it was in fact the original location of the site of so many executions, including her own.

My own research into the life and times of Lady Jane Grey shows an incredibly devious and complicated web being spun by various members of the nobility. The events of this time seem just as convoluted as the popular TV series *Game of Thrones*.

Until her subsequent research into these historical figures Sharon had never heard of any of them, except for her childhood association with Lady Jane Grey. When Sharon visited a portrait gallery in England she was drawn to a painting of a woman and immediately felt quite disturbed even though she had no idea who it was. When she asked an attendant the name of the woman he told her that it was Princess Mary, also known as 'Bloody Mary'. When Sharon later found out after her regression that it was Mary who had sentenced Lady Jane to death, it all fell into place for her.

Sharon's story is a wonderful example of our intuition opening our mind to a potential link to the past. The fact that she went on to unveil the whole past-life connection confirms the message of trust that later emerged from her regression into the life and times of Lady Jane Grey.

***

Several months after my first interview with Sharon Prince, I invited John Davis to a guest appearance on *RadioOutThere* to get details straight from the horse's mouth, or maybe in this instance the apostle's mouth.

In this lifetime John was raised in a strict Catholic family and went through the process of being an altar boy as part of his religious upbringing. So when Sharon told him in his reading that he is the reincarnation of the apostle John, also known as John the Beloved, it came as a huge shock to John Davis. He literally ran away after this disclosure and refused to have any contact with Sharon for six months. John recalled he was scared when given the news, not because of what he was told but because of how he felt at that time. 'When I heard those words I knew it was true. We all know the truth in our heart, and that scared me more than anything else.'

John explained that during his Catholic upbringing the subject of reincarnation was 'not really smiled upon … nor are psychics smiled upon'. With this perspective of his religious background, everything about Sharon's revelation of his past was wrong. He ran away because, as he put it, 'I didn't want to be the odd man out, but eventually spirit turned me around and put me back on my path.'

John then came into contact by one means or another with 13 different psychics who all told him the same story, reinforcing what he had been told earlier: he is the reincarnation of a man who walked with Jesus.

John particularly remembers the second psychic who confirmed his past incarnation as John the Beloved. 'She is certified with Edgar Cayce's Association for Research and Enlightenment,' he told me, and her information and credibility made a big impression on him.

In the interview, I asked John whether at any time he doubted this information even though it came from so many different and independent sources. Could it have even been some sort of trickery? He replied that at the time of meeting Sharon Prince he was a very science-based person and had a lot of serious questions about the whole episode. So he decided to call a few psychics out of the blue to make sure there was no chance of collusion. The psychics who made the greatest impact were the ones who rushed up to him in crowds to grab him by the arm and tell him of his past life without any kind of prompting or prior contact.

John has rationalised that as we are all connected and have access to the divine, when information has to be shared from source it is done through many people. After his contact with the 13 psychics confirmed his inner feelings, John decided to go one step further and have a past-life regression with a certified regressionist. John's session went for an hour and a half, and he recalled meeting Jeshua for the first time on a beach. He addressed him as 'rabbi'; being raised a Catholic, in hindsight John found this 'a little amusing'. John described Jeshua primarily as a teacher, 'an embodiment of all our potential. He was here to show us the way, the truth and the life we are all capable of achieving. '

John described himself as being normally a very visual person, but this regression took him into another space entirely. 'It was as if I was actually standing there on that beach feeling all the sensory awareness of being there. He [Jeshua] was standing about six or eight feet away from me and I could feel his presence. I could literally feel the unconditional love coming from the man.'

Meanwhile the regressionist, who was watching this but didn't know what John was experiencing, asked the question: 'Are you with him or are you him?' John responded, 'I am within him.' He explained that feeling as being at one with Jeshua.

John had often wondered during his religious upbringing why the apostles just gave up their lives and walked away to follow Jeshua. His answer was provided when the regressionist asked John what was happening at this time and his reply came: 'He gave me a glimpse of everything and now I have to be with him.'

I put it to John Davis in the interview that as someone raised a strict Catholic his subconscious may have created the visions in his regression to provide the answers he was seeking at that time.

John admitted that a lot of people have asked him the same question, along with making accusations that he is in contact with the devil. As a scientifically minded man, John started looking for proof of his experience on the beach. He remembers being told by the regressionist to look down at himself and seeing bare arms and legs but thinking that the apostles all wore robes. His subsequent research revealed details of what he described as a 'fisher's coat', which was basically a one piece Galilean bathing suit. As John said, 'If you fall in the water wearing robes, you are going to be dragged under and drown.' He later discovered in the Bible a reference to Peter when seeing Jeshua after he rose: Peter 'put on his fisher's coat and jumped into the water, because he was fishing naked'.

John also recalled seeing an image of the boat he was using when he first met Jeshua, describing a C-shaped hook located on a spire at the front of the boat. John described it as being about 30 centimetres across, and said he had never seen anything like it during this lifetime. His research revealed that when fishermen at that time were casting their nets off the side of the boat they would take the draw line and put it through the C-shaped hook. They would then pull the line from the other side so it would draw the net up beside the boat.

A fascinating part of the regression happened when John was instructed by the regressionist to go to the scene of the crucifixion. John described 'very specifically seeing these short, multi-tailed whips that had a fishtailed-shaped handle, and I saw these beads on the tail'. John subsequently verified that these beads were part of the whipping process referred to by the Romans as scourging.

Despite this evidence John said he still struggled with the whole question of his past life, and 'on multiple occasions asked for signs' to be given to him to further it verify and make sure he was not deluding himself.

'It was so far outside of everything I was taught; and to feel that unconditional love in such a very real way, it was a very real experience for me.' John was also struck by the memory of referring to the man as Jeshua throughout the whole experience, never having referred to him as anything but Jesus in this life.

John went on to say that every time he asked for a sign it was given to him. 'The last time I asked I was driving down the road and I had just gone through a traumatic experience with my wife.' Wondering once again whether he was deluding himself with this whole reincarnation thing, he asked for just one more sign. He came to a red light, looked to the right and saw a billboard being erected. 'It was pure white and they had just put the first two words in the centre, which said "SAINT JOHN". I asked for a sign and He literally gave me a sign!'

We both had a good laugh at that, and John summed up the reaction he got from source beautifully: 'Come on: thirteen psychics and a regression, what more do you want?'

After John Davis accepted his past life as the apostle John his life was changed forever. His natural abilities as a healer were brought out during a talk he was presenting in Houston, Texas, when the organiser asked him to give healing to a woman in the audience. As she came to the front of the room John saw an image of an angel standing behind her, and not knowing what to do next said he would pray for healing for her. As he closed his eyes and asked the woman to do the same, he felt the energy of Jeshua standing behind him, the same energy he experienced in his regression. He clairvoyantly saw Jeshua walk past him towards the woman. There were other clairvoyants and psychics in the audience, and two of them later reported seeing Jeshua's image next to John. Sharon Prince was sitting next to John at the time and also felt Jeshua's energy as he walked between them.

John went on to say: 'I watched him walk over to the lady and put his hands on her hands, and at the time she thought they were my hands touching her. The next day her lupus had healed.'

That was John's first healing experience. He had participated in hundreds of healings by the time of our interview, which was recorded around 10 years ago. He has witnessed everything from someone with six weeks to live with cancer being healed overnight, muscular dystrophy being healed in five minutes, brain tumours being healed instantly, tumours on the back of the head melt an hour after the healing, and many other examples of amazing healings. But John summed it up with the words Jeshua always said to him: 'It's your faith that always heals you.'

John realised at this stage of his life that he was at the very beginning of his spiritual work and his life would never be the same again.

My interview with John took place in 2009; we have not been in contact since then, despite both Sharon Prince's and my own efforts to get in touch. My research showed that he is currently working as a corporate action hero and trainer, embracing practical and spiritual ideals.

This quote from a website interview with John Davis by Edie

Weinstein (https://bit.ly/2N1OaD1) may explain his decision to embrace the past and move on with his mission in this life:

> I feel privileged to have those memories, but I am very clear that it is all me. They are just earlier memories. One lesson I received in this amazing journey, is that it does not matter who anyone was in a past life. It only matters what you are doing right here, right now. Many people hear about my past life experiences and want to associate me as a holy man or an apostle. I am just a person like any other person, as you are. I feel we are each on our own journey and how we live our lives through thought, word, and deed is what matters.

Chapter 14

ANGELS, GUIDES, DOGS AND OTHER WORLDS

Are there such beings as angels, and what is their place in the cycle of reincarnation?

My spokespirit John Dingwall, when replying to this question from the world of spirit, confirmed that angels have a different energy to humans. 'They are different but also part of that tapestry that makes up the universal fabric of life.'

He became very reflective and was obviously having this information shared from other members of his afterlife spirit group, which he described as being more advanced in the world of spirit. 'People like to be able to put labels on everything, because if you can't put a name to something how are you going to picture it in your mind's eye? Angels have their place; it's another form of nurturing, a healing energy, particularly used in times of shock and trauma.'

I shared with John that I often call on my angels for help, which is invariably given. He replied that our spirit guides most usually appear in the form of angel energy, and this could be the reason for their helpful presence. My own guide confirmed later that there is an energy crossover at times and some very advanced guides do indeed have angelic energy. Angels have never incarnated, and these advanced guides are no longer required to reincarnate as they have completed their life cycle.

John confirmed what my other research has revealed: that we do not always just return to Earth for our next life but do take on lives in other worlds. This is not just because a soul is bored by earthly life and wants new experiences, as a change of direction like this has to be earned. The decision about future life forms is made in consultation with our guides and higher spiritual energies when we return to the afterlife. Many people have memories of lives on other worlds, and I look closely at this in Chapter 21.

Out of the blue, John casually mentioned that we do not always return to Earth as human beings. This gave me quite a shock, as I had always believed that once a human energy always a human energy, and returning as an animal would be a retrograde step.

'You can come back as an animal, in a certain form, a slightly different energy.' My first reaction was to question whether this was a retrograde step in our soul's progress. John's answer surprised me but at the same time made a lot of sense.

'If you come back to teach some lessons in your next life what better way than as a dog, nurturing and helping an elderly person for instance, and to teach as well.' He confirmed it was more likely to be in the form of a teaching situation than returning as a fly or mosquito. Once again the guides for that particular soul would decide what kind of animal was appropriate for that occasion. John said he mentioned the example of a dog 'because you can imagine the power and the love of a dog. There have to be good reasons because, let's face it, no one ever loved a mosquito!'

Who said they don't enjoy a laugh in the afterlife?

My guides then chimed in by confirming that, despite what some may believe, we are not sent back to earth as a fly or a cockroach as punishment for our previous life's actions or misdemeanours. It is something to feel relieved about next time you thump a cockroach with a rolled up newspaper!

Chapter 15

CASE STUDIES FROM PETER SMITH

W hen I decided to write this book, one of the first people I conferred with was Peter Smith. I was delighted when he later agreed to write the introduction. Peter is regarded as being a leader in spiritual hypnotherapy both in Australia and the United States. He created the Institute of Hypnoenergetics, which blends hypnotherapy, energy and consciousness. An important part of the work of the institute is past-life regression therapy, and Peter has conducted many sessions as well as training new practitioners. He is also the president of the Newton Institute in the US, and is an acknowledged leader in the field of the life-between-lives program begun by the late Michael Newton.

Peter has since passed the mantle of hypnoenergetics to Colleen Dooley in Melbourne, so that he can focus on his new passion in life: quantum consciousness (see Chapter 21 for more on this).

As Peter has been a frequent guest on *RadioOutThere* we have forged a close bond, and when he offered to put me through some past-life regressions for this book I jumped at his offer. He has a natural ability to take his subjects very deep into their subconscious to access their previous lives, just as I was able to experience for the two regressions I have already included in this book. I went so deep that most of the information came as a complete surprise when I listened to the audio recording of the session afterwards. Peter also led me through a private hypnoenergetics course in 2016 to add to my previous regression work, and I found it a rich and very satisfying experience.

Ancient Egypt

Peter has many case studies and offered to release some of the more appropriate regressions for *Past Lives Unveiled*; for the sake of privacy the names of the subjects are not revealed. The first case is with a young woman we will call Rose Foster, who I refer to by her initials RF. Rose was first taken back to the time she was a foetus in her mother's womb. Deep in trance, Rose said that her spirit first entered into her body four months into the pregnancy, and when asked said she was pleased it was an excellent physical match as 'it has positive imprints I can work with'.

> PS (Peter Smith): What are your initial impressions
> about the life you are coming into?
> RF: It will not be easy, with more emotional trauma in
> this life, but I will be helping others from a good
> position.

This early contact shows how the spirit has been prepared for its next life, and has obviously agreed to the 'traumas' that it will entail.

Peter then took RF into an even deeper state of regression, down a tunnel to a past lifetime that would provide a different context and importance to the life about to be embraced. This past lifetime had to be different from any past life she had previously explored. Peter first took her to a significant day she experienced in this lifetime.

RF (jumping immediately into her past life, exclaimed almost breathlessly): 'I'm in Egypt ... It's day, I'm on stone.' (There was a note of surprise in her voice as she continued): 'I'm a dancer. I invoke energy, using body movements.' She seemed to embrace this past life closely for a while before continuing, 'I was killed by L—. He was a priest, supposed to be somebody I could trust.' (L— was apparently somebody significant in RF's current life who had cropped up in previous regressions with Peter.)

PS: Why were you shown this lifetime?

RF: To release a lot of the pain of being murdered. I've already forgiven [him] but there's an energy there that's the reason L— chases me through lives.

PS: Is this energy at his end?

RF: Yes. There's a lot of lust from his end ... by dominating me, by taking me, by using me, he had power [over me].

PS: Is there anything you can do?

RF (in a stronger, more confident voice now): Funnily enough she has done enough in this life, but I wanted her to see it ... to see what it's like. It was time she remembered the way he looks at her.

PS: Who am I speaking with now?

R: Aria, I am the soul.

Peter suggested it would be a positive step for RF to go through the death scene in her life in Egypt to release any remaining traces that may be affecting her current life. He then took RF to her last day in Egypt.

RF (sounding a little wistful): I have a lover, we are very much in love. I've got a feeling today … I know it's my last day, but I don't want to think about that.

PS: Do you recognise your lover as someone in your current life?

RF: Yes. My lover's name was Sshaa.

PS: Now move forward to your last moments in this lifetime.

RF (whispering): I've finished the ceremony, a very powerful one. I know that L— is taking my energy … I'm allowing it to happen … He's touching me. He can take my energy, but he can't take my body. He's tried to seduce me and it's not working. He's starting to get rough … No! I will not allow this to happen. (pause) I'm hitting the ground against the stone … I've lost several teeth. I don't care, he can do what he wants to my being, it's just a body, just a vehicle. He's hitting my head against the stone! (pause) Now I'm outside the body.

As RF, now detached from her body, watches, L— starts to dismember her body. 'He just doesn't know what he's doing.'

Peter takes her to a location far, far above her body, which she describes as 'a place filled with gossamer-like light'. Here her soul partner greets her in an emotional reunion that she describes as 'we are immersed' As she looks around, RF sees 'flickerings of different people' that she recognises from previous lifetimes.

Peter then asked Aria to come through again, enquiring whether she had any previous lives on other worlds. Aria described an earlier life on a world of water, where she lived in a very beautiful place underwater. Aria recalled early memories of this planet that were connected with what we recognise on Earth as a trident, the symbol we associate with the ancient Roman god Neptune. She remembered that the number three was very significant in her association with this world.

> Aria: I think it had three suns, or perhaps three moons. The number three is very important to those beings, and part of the soul memory to bring that into being was the trident.
>
> PS: What kind of beings were on this planet?
>
> Aria: Oh, funny beings … very slim. It was a planet with just an ocean, really. [They were] breathing oxygen from the water – it was very peaceful. This life was far prior to me being human. There was emotion in this life, a lot of emotion.

Aria went on to say that for certain people selected to be born on Earth it was like a preparation so they would be able to cope with the immense amount of human emotion. Still immersed in her watery world, Aria's voice trailed off.

> PS: Where are you now?
>
> Aria: I'm just exploring that planet, remembering back [to that life].

Peter then took Aria back to the spirit world and her life as RF. By now Aria had merged with the soul energy she used in that lifetime as RF and was once again a complete soul.

> PS: Now where are you in the spirit world, what are you doing?
>
> Aria: Meeting with the wise ones.
>
> PS: Tell me what the wise ones are saying.
>
> Aria: This is all just a drama; we like to take on roles.
>
> PS: Ask the leader of the wise ones what is expected of RF in this lifetime.
>
> Aria: [The leader says] I am doing well, I am utilising the body well. It is important to give up addictions [smoking] as it does have a karmic significance.
>
> PS: The purpose of this lifetime?
>
> Aria: To spark people. There could still be an early exit, which is connected to my fears, because of my last incarnation when I went out very young. This

may not be a very old, old life, but they are going
to leave some surprises in there yet.

PS: Spark people? How?

Aria: Energy to do with my very being. I use my eyes
and people remember who they see.

PS [knowing that we only bring a certain amount of
our soul energy into each life]: What percentage
of your soul energy did you bring back this time?

Aria: They're showing me twelve, but that seems very
low. No wonder I get tired.

Aria spoke about working with a large soul group in the afterlife
whose mission it was to help with the evolution of consciousness
on Earth. She said she has only ever incarnated with some of these
souls, while the others work from the world of spirit. Aria went on
to say that some of these souls are engaged in healing the planet
directly, in what she describes as 'very important times now'. She
also mentioned that some members of this soul group are what we
would describe as aliens, but they have been in the world of spirit
for ages.

Obviously it was important for RF to understand and be able to
release the negative energy that L— had had over her in various
lifetimes. It also demonstrates how we can get caught up in power
struggles with somebody who has control over us in our current
incarnation. By releasing the past we are able to break free from
these chains and regain the power we need to lead a fulfilled life.

A very interesting revelation in RF's regression was the story of her incarnation on a watery world prior to beginning her cycle of lives on Earth. The experience of dealing with the intense emotions we have in our lives here is obviously an important factor in cases where we will eventually be required to help others in a key future life. RF is now working with large numbers of people in her professional work, helping them heal past wounds — many of which involve intense emotions — so they may find their true purpose.

A simple but meaningful past-life study

Many people like to fantasise they will regress to a lifetime with a colourful, even romanticised storyline, like that in a Hollywood movie. However, in most cases regressions look back at simple but meaningful events in very ordinary circumstances that have relevance to our current life. The main purpose of our life cycles is to have every experience deemed necessary by spirit for our advancement as a soul. As we so often travel with many of the same people from lifetime to lifetime, this can mean an accumulation of karma that needs to be cleared before we can progress to the ultimate stage where we don't have to reincarnate on Earth.

Many of us also agree to help others from past lives play out their karma or have new experiences by playing a key role in their lives. When I look at this scenario from my own background, it is as if we are all part of a gigantic touring theatrical production that just keeps getting bigger and more complicated as the years roll by. Each new life is like an actor who takes on a new character to keep developing and furthering their career.

Such is our next case study of Grace Martin, as we'll call her. Peter initially took Grace back to her time in the womb. She recalled coming and going several times from the world of spirit before she finally stayed with her new body a few days before the actual birth. Peter took Grace to the past life best connected to her current incarnation, and asked her to describe whether it was day or night time.

> GM: Daylight, and I'm outside.
> PS: Look down at your feet and tell me what you see.
> GM: Bare feet … I'm standing on shingles with wet
>   legs. I'm by myself, but I can hear other people.
>   I'm female … long fair hair, pale skin, wearing a
>   yellow dress … It's kind of pulled up.

When asked for more details about herself, GM remembered that her name was Sarah Hopkins and the year was 1918. Sarah lived in Texas in the United States and was at a picnic by the river.

> PS: What's the purpose of the picnic?
> GM: It's my mother's birthday.

Peter asked Sarah for more details about herself.

> GM: I'm nineteen and I have a brother. I've finished
>   school and I live at home.
> PS: Tell me about your family home.

GM: It's a little house just out of town. My father works in a store in the town.

Peter then took Sarah forward in time to a significant event.

GM: I'm in my house with children. I'm thirty-two years old and have three children, aged seven, four and two.

PS: I want you to tap into the energy of your children. Do you know them from your life as Grace? Start with your seven year old.

GM: These are different children. I don't know these children.

PS: Tell me about your husband; do you recognise him?

GM: (surprised): 'It's C—.' [Her husband in this life]

PS: What's his name in this lifetime?

GM: Peter.

Peter Smith then took Grace forward to the next significant event.

GM: I'm looking after C—; he's sick.

It is interesting to note that even though she has regressed to a past life, Grace still associates with the energy of her husband in her current life.

PS: How old are you?

GM: Fifty-three … fifty-four; I'm not sure.

PS: How sick is he?

GM: Very sick, he's got pneumonia … I think he's dying. My youngest daughter is helping me look after him.

Peter moved GM forward in time and asked if he survived.

GM: No, he's gone.

Peter took her further forward in time, asking if she was still in Texas.

GM: Yeah. I'm now sixty, or sixty-one … I've got really sore legs, I can't walk around. I'm in bed … it's an illness. I don't know what's wrong, the doctors don't tell me anything … It's getting worse, creeping up … It's in my hips now.

Peter tells Sarah to go to the time when her soul left the body.

GM: Hard to breathe … I'm still in bed. I feel as if I don't want to go.

PS: What's keeping you in the body?

GM: My daughter is still there, looking after me. She doesn't want me to go … but I have to go.

Sarah described her soul leaving her body, now free from pain. Her soul heads upwards and she is able to look back at Earth, feeling reluctant to cross over. She wasn't sure when she would be back on Earth, or to be honest if she ever wanted to return. Peter now started to directly communicate with Sarah's soul energy and asked her to look back on the life she had just left to see what she had learned.

> GM: Something to do with loyalty. It's about staying with people.
>
> PS: How did that manifest with Sarah?
>
> GM: She was going to leave her husband, but she stayed.
>
> PS: Why did she stay?
>
> GM: Obligation.
>
> PS: How does that relate to the life as Grace?
>
> GM: In this life she left him ... It was a backward step.
>
> PS: What else was important in Sarah's life?
>
> GM: As Sarah I didn't like being with my parents, that's why I was with Peter. I wanted to leave my parents.

It would seem from this revelation that in this life Grace had to complete unresolved karma from at least one past life with her current husband as one of the prime reasons for this incarnation.

Looking at the timeline it appears it was only a few Earth years after leaving her body as Sarah that she was reborn as Grace. I asked

Peter if this could be a special set of circumstances, as my research has indicated we usually spend some time in the afterlife before reincarnating. Peter said his research and also that of Dr Michael Newton has shown there is no 'normal' length of time before reincarnating, as every soul's journey is unique.

I was surprised when Peter went on to say that Michael Newton had even found in a few of his 7000 or so case studies that the same soul was actually in two bodies at the same time. As I wrote earlier, we do not bring our full soul energy back to our life on Earth, so this is perfectly understandable. In some extreme cases the same soul can experience complete lifetimes in different bodies without ever meeting their 'twin soul'. It must be fascinating for the remaining soul energy in the world of spirit to keep an eye on two entirely different human experiences. It brings new meaning to the old phrase: 'and never the twain shall meet'.

Robbery and murder in mediaeval times

JA was excited about his future when Peter Smith established contact with his soul just prior to his birth in this life. He described it as feeling like he was about to set out, full of expectations, on a holiday. It was going to be a great opportunity to 'really get in and experience life to the full this time'. JA's spirit joined the foetus a little earlier than normal, as he remembers he was 'raring to go!'

When asked how he felt about the body he was going to use in this life JA said it was going to be big, which really suited his purpose. He knew that his body would be athletic and have a lot of durability.

Peter took JA deeper into his regressed state to a scene in a significant past life and asked him to describe his surroundings and appearance. JA went easily back to a time where he found himself in a rural setting 'surrounded by pastures'. He was wearing boots covered in mud, pants made from a coarse fabric, and a 'cloak shirt-like thing' on top. When asked to step away and describe his physical features, JA said he was a man who looked pretty weathered, a bit dirty, had whiskers and was aged about 30. He was walking and heading in the direction of 'a house, or barn or somethin' '.

Now inside a small house where he lived, JA expanded on his profile as being a self-sufficient farmer who lived alone in England in the 1500 or 1600s. Peter took him forward a little in time, where JA spoke about eating his dinner. It was warm inside his little home, with a fire burning brightly, and he was eating a kind of stew he'd made along with some bread that he recalled was 'funny, hard bread'.

JA's meal was disturbed by the sound of horses approaching, and the next thing two men appeared at his doorway. He recalled the scene vividly: 'I don't know them, but they just walk in. They're not very nice people and they want to rob me.' While JA watched on helplessly, one of the men helped himself to the plate of stew on the table and then started looking around the small house.

'He pushed things off the shelf near the fireplace, to see if there was anything valuable there that he could steal.' JA tried to stay positive, saying he had the feeling the men were running from something and just want somewhere to eat and sleep and then leave. However, he was taken by surprise when one of the men turned and stabbed him unexpectedly, with no provocation. He was severely wounded and died a few minutes later.

Peter asked if he recognised either of the men from his current life as JA. 'They seem familiar, but I can't place them,' he replied. By now JA's spirit is detached from his body, and when he looked at it on the ground he became really angry. 'It was such a lonely life. I tried to do everything right, and I just get killed … nothing!' he mutters loudly. 'It was just like time wasted, it was unfair.'

Peter took him deeper into a soul state immediately after that unfortunate lifetime. JA was still feeling disappointment at the way he died. As he started to rise upward, JA couldn't look back at the Earth he had just left as it was obscured by what he described as white smoke. He had the feeling of having to keep moving in an upward direction as he headed home to the peaceful realm of the world of spirit. As he arrived JA was joined by his guide, who he referred to as 'Mahtok'. Peter asked if he could communicate with Mahtok about the life JA had just completed. 'Of course,' came the reply.

Peter enquired about the direct relationship in that time to his current life, asking why he went to that particular life. Mahtok laughed and told JA's soul energy that he already knew the answer to that question. Mahtok then explained that 'not every life is expected to be bells and whistles. You have every life for experience; nothing more, nothing less.'

Peter still wanted to dig deeper: 'But why that particular one; how does it relate back to JA?'

Mahtok was quick with his reply: 'Because it was simple; he was lonely. In his current life JA takes for granted not being lonely.' Peter asked whether that was the only lesson or if there were more.

'You should never feel that you are owed anything, because if you think you have already earned it you can do as you will.' Mahtok's words seem enigmatic at first, but were obviously carefully said to make JA reflect on certain aspects of his current life.

When Peter asked what happened next on his return to the afterlife, Mahtok replied that he was taking JA's soul energy to a room where he would be reunited with many familiar spirits who were laughing and seemingly enjoying themselves. JA was obviously still angry about his recent demise, and his companions told him not to be so serious about the life he had just completed as it was all over now.

Peter asked JA if he recognised any of the spirits from his current life, and he confirmed there were a couple of familiar faces. When prompted by Peter, JA asked one of them to come forward. He recognised someone that he called Paul from his current life: 'It was funny when he came out of the crowd and was moving to the front, it was like he was shy. He did that so I would recognise him from this life.' JA revealed that his friend referred to him in the world of spirit as 'Shahree, or something like that'. Paul told JA that he worried too much, mainly about silly things. He added that JA needed to relax in his current life.

Peter then focused on communicating with Shahree to find out more about JA's soul energy and current life purpose. Shahree revealed he was part of a smaller soul group of 'maybe five or ten', who were a really close group that he was then working with.

'I am actually helping them more than they are helping me. They have some dramas that are repetitive; they keep doing the same things. I'm like another piece in the chess set and we play certain roles to change the way it works. They keep dying before they make each other happier.'

Shahree saw a couple in his group who have reunited in this life, but said nothing had changed for them. 'One has died ... They keep missing the point. They are both very scared: scared to make it work, scared things will fail between them if they actually commit to do something together. That's on Earth, but here they are different ... so different. They keep being given challenging lives, each of them in different ways, and they falter. They think of what could go wrong as opposed to what could go right.'

Peter asked Shahree what his role was in helping these people overcome their problems. 'They are supposed to see the difference,' Shahree replied. 'We've tried a few different ways, but it hasn't worked.'

When asked who these people were, Shahree identified three people in JA's life that were present in the crowd of souls surrounding him — including H—, a soul he has had problems with for some time. Shahree said H— was selected to come into this group to help out, the same way others have helped him in past lives. However, H— treated JA as an outsider, which only added to the difficulty.

This is a classic example of a person reincarnating to play an important role in the karmic dramas of other souls in their group. It illustrates how our lives on Earth are usually a combination of our own individual learning experiences as well as working with others to assist them in resolving their karma from previous lives. It is all part of the intricate tapestry of life for evolution of our souls. Once again, it is like the cast in a play or a film all playing their parts in the story as it unfolds.

The question about the number of lives we have led is one often asked by people enquiring about their past lives. When asked this question Shahree said: 'Lots: sixty or seventy.' He added that he has not lived on 'other worlds in the Earth universe, but there are many different worlds'. He went on to explain: 'It's like you want to book a holiday, and you get to choose a continent you would like to visit. It's the same thing: Earth is one continent and there are other places as well, just like there are different continents. Each has a different feel about them — different energies — and there are different challenges. Earth's challenge is people, people in conflict. It is the heavier out of all of them in terms of energy. People struggle here; there are so many things you can take, but the idea is that you are not supposed to take them. If you keep taking them there's conflict.'

It would seem that when Shahree refers to 'taking' he means not only the removal of material objects, but also adversely affecting the emotional and spiritual lives of others through the various power games and manipulations so evident in our world.

When Peter asked him what JA's primary soul purpose is for this life, Shahree said that he is supposed to help two people, B and K, but one of them has already left. 'So now I'm supposed to help the other person come up with a different way of thinking … That even though there is a loss, it's not over. K is doing better; she still has tendencies to go to pieces, but it's not as bad [now].'

Peter asked Shahree how he measured the progression of his soul. 'It's what you do for other people. People are always doing things for you, but you might not notice it. That's how you learn. It's like driving a car: you practise.'

Peter then asked at what stage of evolution Shahree was as a soul, to which he replied: 'I think I'm fairly high up. I don't like being high up. I prefer working lower; that's where the challenge is.' Shahree went on to say that his job was to help people progress in little groups in small ways. 'It's not a massive effort, just a little concentrated one.'

Shahree seems to be identifying here an ongoing commitment to help other souls over several lifetimes. He then revealed that one of his other 'jobs' was to help protect newer souls who needed lots of nurturing, 'otherwise they can crack'. He achieves this by watching and listening to them. My impression at this point of the regression is that Shahree was fairly close to having the status of a guide, and was mainly working with other souls in this incarnation as his prime purpose.

Shahree then spoke about children in this lifetime that he referred to as the 'crystals'. He described them as being 'older souls coming to change the spin of the way it [the world] is going, to slow it down, to simplify it. It's too much, too frantic. All the creative energy is going into creating a hectic space, a heavy space. There are many of these souls; they are everywhere. They are here to heal, like a spring cleaning.'

Asked about the patterns of his past incarnations, Shahree answered: 'I've done a lot, I've lived a lot of lives. I keep coming back to Earth; for me it's the most enjoyable space, like a habit.' He revealed that he brought back what he termed 'a fair whack of energy' to this lifetime, as he didn't know how things would turn out. When questioned further, a fair whack turned out to be just under 50 per cent, which was more than he usually brought back. He reasoned that if he needed it he could draw on this extra energy.

The other part of his soul energy is still in the world of spirit, 'studying, looking ahead and creating future lives'. When asked about future incarnations, Shahree said: 'There will be as many as I need to, or want to [have].' He concluded the regression by adding: 'I don't need to keep coming back but I like it here, and there are things I can do for others. JA needs to keep it simple, as he has a penchant for indulgence.'

Shahree's final comments indicate there is a degree of choice about reincarnating. My contacts in the afterlife say the choice is made by advanced spirits in the Council of Elders, along with our principal guide. However, ultimately it's really up to each individual to reach that stage of their soul evolution where there is no need to return. This means that my previous thoughts about Shahree being a 'guide in training' or something similar could be true if he 'likes it here' and can help others.

Chapter 16

THE STRANGE REINCARNATION OF NORMAN SHEALY

Psychologist and author Dr Michael Newton's case studies into life between lives disclose that we are usually given certain choices about the body we are going to work with in our next incarnation. Once our soul understands its main purpose in the next life we are allowed to have a say in the physical body we are about to be given, often including the gender. While we could be forgiven for believing we would all want to return with film star appearances, this is not the case. The bodies on offer are those deemed appropriate for each individual and their future circumstances. I would surmise that genetics would also play a role.

Given that there is an element of choice, why would a soul choose or accept a body with severe physical, mental or emotional problems, or indeed harsh family or environmental situations? The answer is both simple and logical. As our lives on Earth are part of what has been referred to as a 'testing ground', accepting some kind of handicap can be one of the most effective ways to clear ongoing karmic conditions and take a giant leap in the evolution of the soul.

The story of Dr Norman Shealy stands out as being something completely different. His choice of physical body in this incarnation is unique, to say the least. Walter Semkiw MD included this extraordinary case in his book *Born Again* (Pluto Project, 2007). Walter and Norman kindly agreed to allow this story to be published here, detailing evidence of a current life taking up the reins from a previous one.

Norman Shealy was born on 4 December 1932 in the US city of Columbia, South Carolina. He began studying medicine at the age of 19 and is now a world-famous neurosurgeon, specialist in pain management, writer and inventor. He invented the TENS unit, which discharges an electrical current through the skin to block pain. He also invented the dorsal column stimulator and developed facet Rrhizotomy, both of which help to reduce or manage back pain.

In 1972 Dr Shealy went to Aspen, Colorado to attend a lecture by Dr William Kroger at the Neuroelectric Society. He recalls being annoyed at Kroger's insistence that acupuncture was hypnosis; but when Kroger spoke about a 19th-century British physician named John Elliotson, who maintained he could operate on patients who were mesmerised (an early form of hypnosis), Norman Shealy's life changed forever.

'I felt as if someone had thrust an iceberg down my back and I said to myself, my God, that's me.' Shealy described himself as being neutral about reincarnation at that time, but was motivated to find out as much as he could about Elliotson. He decided to travel to the United Kingdom for the answers he was seeking.

Arriving in London, Shealy hailed a cab and asked to be taken to the Royal College of Surgeons, as he felt that Elliotson had to have been a surgeon. This is where his life took another sudden turn. 'I was sitting in the back of the cab and suddenly was picked up physically and turned in the opposite direction, again feeling as if there "were an iceberg down my back". A block down to the left, instead of the right, was the University College Hospital of London.' Shealy told the taxi driver to change direction, and when he got out he went into the building he had observed he immediately felt at home. As he delved into the past, Shealy found out details that amazed him. He discovered that Elliotson was the first professor of medicine at the University College Hospital, where his office was located. From here Elliotson established his reputation in the 1830s by giving public lectures.

During his medical career Elliotson introduced the stethoscope to British medicine and also the use of narcotics, both of which were being used in France at that time. He also started working with mesmerism, conducting public displays in the amphitheatre.

Outside his medical practice Elliotson became good friends with two of the leading writers of the day, Charles Dickens and William Thackeray. He showed Charles Dickens how to use mesmerism on his wife, who was a hypochondriac. He also demonstrated that, when placed in a mesmeric trance, some of his patients became clairvoyant and were able to diagnose medical problems in other patients. It was a matter of course that Elliotson would upset the medical authorities with these unorthodox practices. When the Board of Studies ordered him to stop holding public displays of mesmerism Elliotson became angry and resigned.

However, because of his contributions to medicine he was later invited by the Royal College of Physicians to give the Harveian Oration, an annual lecture that started in 1656. Being a very strong-willed individual, Elliotson took this opportunity to speak out against the establishment. The subject of his lecture was 'The Hypocrisy of Science in Accepting New Thoughts'. That would certainly have ruffled a few feathers in those ultra-conservative times, as indeed it might even today.

The deeper Norm Shealy went into John Elliotson's background the more amazed he became about the similarities with his own life. He discovered that Elliotson had black curly hair and walked with a congenital limp. He was also the first physician in London to stop wearing knee-length pants, known as knickerbockers.

Shealy remembered that when he was around four years of age he wanted black curly hair so much that he cut off some of his aunt's black hair. He also told everyone at that time he was going to be a physician. To add to the story, the nine-year-old Shealy refused to wear knee-length pants and threw temper tantrums when his mother tried to make him wear them, tearing them apart. He also fractured his right tibia (shin bone), which led to an infection. The doctors told him he would always walk with a limp. At the age of 16, Shealy dyed his hair black when he went to college. To complete the circle, Elliotson graduated medical school at age 19, the same age Shealy began his medical studies.

Norm Shealy describes Charles Dickens as being one of his favourite authors as a child. In 1974 he visited a well-known healer,

Olga Worrall, who put him under hypnosis. While in the trance, he remembers seeing Olga walk across the room, pick up a book and then put it down again. He rang the healer later, and she told him the name of the book was *Pendennis*, by William Thackeray. Shealy later found out that Thackeray dedicated his 1850 novel to John Elliotson, basing his character Dr Goodenough on Elliotson.

Both Shealy and Elliotson hated medical hypocrisy. Six months before he even heard Elliotson's name, Shealy anonymously published a novel based on the hypocrisy of medicine in accepting new ideas. Unwittingly, he used much of the material that Elliotson had used as part of his Harveian Lecture. At least Shealy can't be accused of plagiarism, as it's difficult to steal your own ideas — even if they were from a past life. A further link between Elliotson and Shealy is the language of ancient Rome: Elliotson was a noted Latin scholar, and Shealy won the Latin Medal twice while attending high school.

Norm Shealy has never doubted from the moment he felt that icy blast down his back in 1972 that in a past life he was Dr John Elliotson. A year later he did a test relating to medical intuition with 75 acknowledged authentic clairvoyants. When he told them the story about his past-life association, all 75 agreed wholeheartedly with him.

To reinforce the commonality between the two doctors, note that Elliotson founded the Phrenology Society in London in 1823 to study the brain as being the organ of the mind, researching whether it was possible to determine character traits by examining the shape of a person's skull; while Shealy sees another link to his former life in his decision to go into neurosurgery, which he says is directly connected to the skull. Following his life as John Elliotson, Norm Shealy is also connected to clairvoyance in treating medical situations. He is famous for his work with world-renowned medical intuitive Caroline Myss, with whom he wrote the books *The Creation of Health* and *The Science of Medical Intuition.* Interestingly, after many years of working individually they reunited for a workshop in 2017.

There is one notable difference between these two lives. Shealy has spent much of his medical career in getting people *off* narcotics, which perhaps is an unresolved karma from his life as John Elliotson, who *introduced* narcotics to British medicine.

The question of physical features being potentially linked to a past incarnation is normally very difficult to prove. However, in the case of Shealy and Elliotson, photographic evidence would appear to put this question beyond doubt. Consider the picture below of Shealy, which was taken when he was a medical student. As the old saying goes: 'A picture is worth a thousand words.'

When I first read about the link between these two outstanding doctors, my first reaction was that Norm Shealy certainly had unfinished business from his previous life as John Elliotson. The feeling of an iceberg going down his back would indicate that higher spiritual energies were in play to guide Shealy to his predestined path as the reincarnation of his former self.

It is an intriguing story, and one that opens many new avenues of possibilities as we lift the veil on the past. Elliotson died in 1868 at the age of 76, and there was a period of 64 years before Shealy was born in 1932. Given the striking resemblance between the two

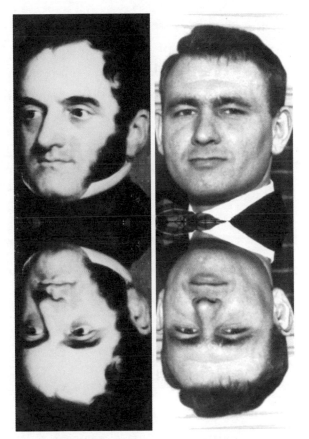

**Doctor
John
Elliotson**

**Doctor
Norm
Shealy**

men, I was not surprised when Norm Shealy told me in an interview on *RadioOutThere* there was not another life in the intervening period.

This is just one example of other people reporting a close physical resemblance to who they were in a past life. Walter Semkiw has included further case studies in *Born Again*. However, as photography has only been available since the 19th century, it is difficult to say how widespread this phenomenon is. Even with photographic evidence taken into account, images from a past life may not be available as they were only used by a small part of the population in the early days.

Who knows how many others there are around the world who may have similar stories to Norm Shealy?

Chapter 17

ARNALL BLOXHAM: A MASSACRE AND A HIGHWAYMAN

Arnall Bloxham is still regarded as being one of Britain's most experienced and respected hypnotherapists. Born in 1881, Bloxham first began experimenting with hypnotic past-life regression in the 1940s. He was elected president of the British Society of Hypnotherapists in 1972, and went on from his practice in Wales to regress some 400 people to examine their past lives.

One of his best subjects, Jane Evans (a pseudonym), experienced six past lives, some of them containing intriguing historical facts about which she could not have possibly known. The most fascinating regression was in the year 286 CE when she was Livonia, the wife of Titus, a tutor in poetry, Greek and Latin to Constantine, who would later become emperor of Rome. Professor Brian Hartley of Leeds University, a specialist in Roman history, checked the details Jane gave Bloxham in the regression and found them to be mainly accurate. An interesting sidelight about this particular past life is that, if it is true, Constantine would have been in Britain in the year 286 CE, which is one of the missing years of his early life, so it is possible that Jane Evans has revealed a detail that has eluded historians.

The York Massacre

Once Bloxham's subjects came to prominence in Wales in the 1970s, he soon came under media spotlight. Jane Evans was persuaded to be regressed in front of television cameras. In deep trance, she went back to a former life as Rebecca, a young Jewish mother in 12th-century York in England, reliving a horrific memory. Rebecca was a simple girl who sold fruit and vegetables in the market place near what she called the 'Cathedral of York', now known as York Minister. Her husband, Joseph, was a moneylender, and they had two children. She was very nervous at this stage of her life because of violence against Jews in nearby Chester and Lincoln, as well as in London.

Rebecca said the locals despised Jewish people, for their clothing, their religious beliefs and customs but most of all for their presumed wealth. She recalled her husband lending money to a man she named Mabelise, who later refused to pay it back. When Joseph took Mabelise to the court of the Assizes, Mabelise became angry and turned on them. A few years later the local populace was goaded into a religious frenzy against the Jewish population, who became terrified for their lives. Rebecca and her daughter Rachel joined a group hiding in the crypt of a local church near the castle in which they had taken sanctuary when the Royal Constable was called away. However, the mob came baying for blood accompanied by soldiers and broke into the church. The priest only escaped with his life by revealing their hiding place; Rebecca described in horrifying detail to the cameras what happened next.

All in all the entire Jewish community of York, some 150 people, perished in the castle keep as well as the crypt in the year 1190. This event was part of what became known in the history books as the 'York Massacre'. (For more details see *More Lives Than One?*, Jeffrey Iverson, Souvenir Press Ltd, 1976.)

Rebecca's memories provided specific information, and when investigated proved historically accurate. Following the telecast, Professor Barrie Dobson identified the church where the massacre took place as being St Mary's in Castlegate, on the outskirts of York. Professor Dobson was a specialist in Jewish history at York University at the time, and the author of a book on the massacre. He stated that many of the details that emerged during the hypnotic session were available only to specialist scholars and were not known by the general public. In other words, Jane Evans could not possibly have known these detailed facts.

However, an even more interesting development later emerged from the regression.

At the time of Jane's regression it was thought that St Mary's Church did not have a crypt, as crypts were rare in York. During church renovations an ancient crypt was discovered on the site that dated back to either the Norman or the Roman period. This discovery confirmed an important detail of the past-life recall not available through any other source (https://bit.ly/2ws2Dky).

To cap off Jane's past-life recall, it turned out that one of the chief instigators of the massacre was one Richard *Malebisse*, who was later fined and banished for his actions. He and his co-conspirators created the havoc so they could escape having to pay back money owed to several Jewish moneylenders.

Jane's memory of the man whom her husband had taken to court without doubt proved to be *Mabelise*, a name virtually identical to Malebise and much too close to be a coincidence.

Life as a notorious highwayman

Roger Cook is a very well-known radio and TV investigative journalist in the United Kingdom. During the many hundreds of programs he has presented he has helped expose villains of all shapes and sizes to the authorities and the general public alike. His investigations include organised crime, drug smuggling, child pornography, people trafficking and the exploitation of endangered animals, among many others.

The cover notes on Roger's autobiography, *Dangerous Ground* (HarperCollins, 1999; reprinted by The Book Guild, 2007), describe his activities and the impact they had on his life.

'For more than twenty-five years Cook exposed a breadth of institutional incompetence, bad law, injustices and naked criminality. During this time he was knocked unconscious a dozen times, required hospital treatment on almost thirty occasions and had a score of bones broken by those who have resented his ruthless persistence, or just objected to the fact that he existed at all. Cook made physical and journalistic fearlessness his trademark.'

Roger Cook is also my oldest and dearest friend, and I was given the honour of appearing as part of his life story in the UK TV production *This is Your Life*.

His journalistic career has quite understandably made him very sceptical of many activities and beliefs, including my own work in the spiritual and metaphysical fields; we agree to disagree on these subjects. However, this has in no way affected our friendship, as Roger has always respected my work — even when I wrote in my book *No Goodbyes* about a past-life regression that took me back to ninth-century Central America and revealed I was a tribal healer and wise woman and Roger was my father.

So it came as quite a surprise when Roger told me about a puzzling experience he had as a reporter for the BBC radio program *The World at One* back in the early 1970s. He'd heard about the famous hypnotherapist Arnall Bloxham, who specialised in past-life therapy, and decided that a feature about Bloxham would be different and eccentric.

'*The World at One* wanted a feature and we'd seen some stuff in a Welsh newspaper about how extraordinary this guy was, so I found his telephone number, contacted him and asked if I could come and interview him. He was reluctant at first because he said he'd never regressed anyone he hadn't selected or recorded himself.'

Roger used his journalistic charm and persuaded Bloxham to be interviewed and so, accompanied by a sound recordist as a witness, drove from London to Wales for the interview.

Roger proved to be a very difficult subject to hypnotise, but eventually went into trance when Bloxham produced an old-fashioned pocket watch and swung it like a pendulum to put him under. Roger describes it as 'succumbing to the cliché of the swinging pocket watch'. Roger remembered a previous occasion when what he describes as a 'very skilled hypnotherapist, Paul Golding, who also had a stage show' had been unable to hypnotise him, even though he was a 'willing victim'. Roger is still not sure whether he was subconsciously blocking the efforts of both hypnotherapists or is just a difficult person to hypnotise.

Once Bloxham had regressed him he asked Roger where he was, and his first words sounded as if he was in 'some kind of daze'. Roger recalls what happened next: 'I began to ramble on about the things I'd done, and I told him about my derring-do adventures, my lucky escapes, my upbringing in a pub in Essex.' Roger was even able to name the pub where he was raised, as well as remembering the names of his mother and father.

'I also told him about stealing a horse called Black Bess, and eventually my hanging at York in 1739.' The recording revealed that as he spoke about the hanging he began to talk in strangulated tones. 'Anyway, it turned out I was Dick Turpin, about whom I knew nothing.'

Dick Turpin is one of England's most notorious 18th-century highwaymen, having started his life of crime in the violent Gregory Gang and later pursuing a solo career.

When Roger got back to London and checked out the colourful career of Turpin, he soon found out he was not the romanticised robber that popular myth has since created. 'I discovered he was a complete shit, and wasn't as according to myth a do-gooder who stole from the rich and gave to the poor.' A thoroughly disappointed Roger Cook learned that Turpin was in fact a poacher, a burglar and a murderer as well as a highwayman. 'When things started to get too hot for him in London, he apparently in 24 hours rode from London to York, changed his name to John Palmer and made his living as a prolific horse thief.' Turpin was eventually caught, tried and hanged at the age of 33 for stealing horses.

Roger still sounds amazed that all the facts that emerged from his regression have proved to be historically correct. 'I also quizzed my sound recordist to see that Bloxham hadn't stopped and started and fiddled things.' The sound recordist said he just sat there and listened while Roger rambled on and nothing untoward happened.

'The only things that didn't check historically were part of myth, in that he didn't ride from London to York in twenty-four hours, which was a Victorian add-on by somebody who wrote a book about highwaymen. The person who did make the ride was somebody else.' Roger also ascertained that there is some dispute about whether the horse was named Black Bess, but everything else all checked out.

Roger described his experience as being as though he had just enjoyed a good meal and a glass of wine and drifted off. He was not conscious of what he said at the time, which was all the more interesting because of the difficulty Bloxham had in hypnotising him. 'It all came as a complete jaw dropper when I heard it played back,' Roger still vividly recalls. Bloxham later told him that very few people remember what they were saying during a regression and it comes as a complete surprise afterwards. This can serve as a good indication of the credibility of past-life regressions.

Roger went to visit Bloxham as a confirmed sceptic about past lives and reincarnation, so what was his reaction when he heard the details of his regression and later confirmed them historically?

'I was absolutely amazed; I couldn't explain it. I'd heard the name

Dick Turpin, but that was all. If you wanted to talk about somebody similar, growing up in Australia, I knew a lot about Ned Kelly.' (Kelly is arguably Australia's most famous bushranger, the Australian equivalent of a highwayman in the 1800s. Kelly, arrested after a legendary gunfight with police and later hanged in 1880, has since become a folk hero.)

Roger agrees that if his subconscious mind had been making up the story of Dick Turpin in his regression, it is logical he would have recreated an outlaw like Ned Kelly instead. However, for Roger after all these years the jury is still out. 'While I simply can't explain it, I still remain to a degree sceptical, because Bloxham's strike rate of famous people was too high. He claims to have found among his regressions Queen Elizabeth and Napoleon.' He added: 'I haven't discounted it. I'm still just sceptical, but you have to allow for the fact that because I'm a journalist I'm a professional sceptic.'

As I wrote earlier, I believe some people do connect with the energy of a famous person so they can learn a valuable lesson for their current life. This does not necessarily mean they themselves were that particular person, but somehow the connection is made for their higher good if they choose to go deeper into its meaning.

One further fact that still has Roger intrigued is that he helped the authorities to bring to justice the United Kingdom's wealthiest and most feared criminal, John Palmer. When Dick Turpin tried to hide from the law in York he changed his name to ... John Palmer!

Coincidence, or was the universe sending a subtle message to Roger Cook about the 18th-century life he once led?

Chapter 18

PHYSICAL IMPACTS FROM THE PAST

There are many ways we can be alerted to past-life events that need to be recognised and cleared during this lifetime so we can move on and be open to positive new experiences.

Seeing red

Judith R, who is well known to me, has a problem that had dogged her for most of her life: she had a violent reaction to the colour red. The mere sight of red in any situation or setting made her nauseous.

In 1999, while recovering from a severe health problem, Judith started sharing an apartment with a young man who worked in the medical field. When he learned of her reaction to red he decided to do something to help her. One night, he arrived home from the hospital where he worked carrying a large piece of cardboard coloured a vivid red. When he told Judith she was to sit and stare at the cardboard, she said she would probably throw up. He got her a bucket, and insisted she just sit looking at the cardboard.

Judith had been recuperating at home from a series of

traumas in her personal life and was spending several hours a day in meditation. She reluctantly agreed to follow her flatmate's instruction, and forced herself to sit and focus on the sheet of red cardboard.

Slipping easily into a meditative state, it wasn't long before a series of visions played across Judith's mind. She saw herself being killed in a series of different events, each of which ended in a bloody death scene. When she focused on the people involved in these visions, Judith recognised the figures of her brother and her ex-husband in this life being actively involved in many of her killings. When she eventually emerged from this trance state Judith felt an immediate sense of relief, as if a giant weight had been lifted from her soul.

From that time on her life began to change. She was able to release the grim evidence of her past lives and instead focus on healing and starting in a new life direction. Judith is now a respected hypnotherapist specialising in trauma resolution work, and is having a positive effect on many people in the global community (https://therichardstraumaprocess.com).

As for the colour red, the nauseous reaction has been relegated to the past and now Judith actually embraces the colour in her life in every possible way.

Déjà vu catalysts

Feeling a strange sense of familiarity with a person you have just met or a place you are visiting can often be associated with past lives. Many people I have spoken with have described an almost eerie feeling of 'having been here before' as they walk down the streets of a town or city apparently for the first time.

In 1992 I went to France to cover the Cannes Film Festival, a long-cherished ambition. At first it was all very exciting, but I soon became disillusioned with the false atmosphere and glitterati and looked for an escape.

A friend of mine, Dee, happened to be travelling with a friend and staying in the nearby colourful port city of Antibes. At the time Dee was working as cabin crew for British Airways, and we had enjoyed some fun times together when she visited my home town of Sydney and helped me celebrate my newly reacquired status of bachelorhood. I went exploring with Dee and her friend in Antibes, and then drove up into the picturesque mountain areas to the north. Dee was on an active search for her own past and asked if I would help her. She believed her key to the past lay in a town called Saint-Paul-de-Vence.

We drove through the spectacular countryside, exploring village after village along the way, until we came to a picturesque place named Tourrettes-sur-Loup, which was a few kilometres from Dee's intended destination. Exploring this charming village with its twisting laneways and quaint houses, we inevitably came to a church that was located in the main square. She insisted we go inside and I naturally followed, although I am not what you call a 'churchy' person. Once inside, we both started to feel a strange sensation of déjà vu. I realised I knew this church from somewhere, and then the visions started.

I 'saw' images of Dee and myself as two nuns who had lived there many years ago. I was told psychically that our life there was in the late part of the 15th century and we had fallen prey to a rather nasty man of the cloth who wanted to have his way with us. The memory gave me the shivers.

Then the most telling part of the vision occurred: I envisioned the church as it had been at that time, which was very different to its current layout. The building we were now standing in was built in a T shape, with the nave at the apex of the T. However, when we were living there in the 15th century it was just a straight rectangular-shaped building, much simpler than the existing church. I also saw that the altar was situated in a different position at that time.

Dee started to really tune in then and came up with a few revelations of her own. She is a very perceptive Scorpio, and her memories felt completely in harmony with my vision. We went outside the church and made our way around to the back of the building and saw that it was quite possible that renovations had been carried out at some time. A spire had been added that Dee felt sure was not there in our previous lives.

Still in our past-life harmonic, we walked a couple of blocks and found the village's historical centre. Sure enough there was a pamphlet available that gave information on the history of the church, written in French and English. It came as a bit of a shock to read that the church had been partially destroyed around 1470 and had to be rebuilt. The rebuilding did not start until 1555, and the new T shape was incorporated into the design.

It all happened around the time of the Cathars and the religious wars that swept that part of France. Further research upon my return to Australia revealed that certain members of the clergy at that time were very corrupt and certainly not averse to a little hanky panky with an attractive nun or two.

At least I assume we were attractive!

After that experience my interest in past lives was piqued. Dee and I went our separate ways, the film festival lost its appeal and the past beckoned me to a different area of France. Before leaving Australia I had purchased a Eurail ticket, which gave me unlimited rail travel, so I proceeded to make full use of this opportunity.

Heading west out of Cannes, I consulted my spirit guide, who had been close by me for the whole trip. Some people use a guide book, while I go for the real thing! My spirit guide at the time asked me to call her Sophie. She told me psychically to initially get off the train at Carcassonne, the beautiful town in south-western France, and I stayed there for a few days. Carcassonne is a fully functioning mediaeval town and was the location for the 1991 film *Robin Hood: Prince of Thieves*, which starred Kevin Costner. I soaked up the atmosphere of the past in this magnificent city before intuitively feeling it was time to move on.

So it was back on the train again for several hours before Sophie told me to get off at the next station at a place I had never heard of, Saint-Nazaire. Located at the mouth of the Loire River, Saint-Nazaire is a port town that seemed to offer few tourist attractions — but Sophie was insistent! In my basic French I asked a taxi driver to take me to a hotel *au bord du mer* (by the sea); however, I ended up at a run-down hotel in the dock area of the waterfront. The owners there were wonderful and treated me as one of the family, which meant I ate my meals in the kitchen with them.

I meditated and asked Sophie why I was there and what was next. I hired a car on her advice and she guided me on a tour of the local area. I had absolutely no idea where I was and the locals spoke no English whatsoever — not even in the tourism office — so it was either put my trust in Sophie or get back on the train. At least I got to learn some new French words.

I am glad I chose the former course of action. It was long before GPS navigation, so Sophie gave me psychic directions to a place I had never heard of before called Guérande. It turned out to be a mediaeval walled city dating back to the sixth century AD, and has a violent and colourful history.

Completely restored, Guérande is now a delightful working town that combines the charm of its colourful past with the comforts of the present day and has lately become a drawcard for tourists visiting Brittany. However, at the time I seemed to be the token tourist, which gave me a unique opportunity to explore free from straggling groups of tourists and umbrella-waving tour guides.

Wandering happily through the charming streets, I put myself completely in Sophie's hands and we ended up in a church (once again). This time it was the Saint-Aubin Collegiate Church; the church dates back to the sixth century, then it went on to become a cathedral in the ninth century.

I walked down the aisle, and apart from Sophie's unseen presence I was alone in this imposing place of worship. The old past-life goose bumps arose as I once again remembered a past life associated with this church. The sensation of walking down the aisle turned into a vision, and I knew I had been married here in a past incarnation. Sophie had brought me back to this place to relive my wedding ceremony, which apparently occurred prior to the French Revolution in the 18th century.

It was a strange feeling, but one that explained so much about my journey through France with my invisible companion. It also offered further proof to me that life is an eternal thread, with each lifetime being part of the patchwork quilt of our soul's evolution. It also explained my fascination with France, its history and its people.

Skip forward 23 years to 2005, when my partner Anne and I were visiting Beijing and we naturally booked a tour to visit and walk on the Great Wall of China. In the coach on the 75 kilometre drive to the wall I suddenly had a vision flash into my mind of the surrounding countryside as it was several hundred years ago. It was very different from how it is today, and I knew then that I had experienced a past lifetime in that region. I managed to speak to our Chinese guide, who confirmed the details of my vision, and I allowed a few old memories to come flooding into my consciousness.

A few minutes later we arrived at the wall, and my vision faded as this amazing place captured my immediate attention. Once we started walking along the parapets I didn't feel any association with the wall itself, and thus have no idea when or exactly where this life took place. All I felt was a strong connection to the surrounding countryside as it was many centuries ago.

Understanding and coming to terms with the past only makes us realise that who and what we are today represents the sum total of all our life experiences. When we do 'die' it is just another step in the very long journey of the spiritual traveller.

Once we open ourselves to the past and accept that our current life is just one of many, it's amazing how déjà vu experiences can crop up unexpectedly from time to time. It is impossible to say if or how many of these experiences or feelings are related to previous lives, but this is just one of the many ways we can unlock our past.

***

In 2006 Anne and I went to New Zealand to join the throngs of people exploring the healing work of John of God. João de Dios, as he is known in his home country of Brazil, was visiting this part of the world for the first time and was attracting large crowds.

John of God is actually a medium who channels the spirits of doctors in the afterlife to help heal those who come to see him. In Brazil he performs both spiritual and physical operations, which I witnessed on a large scale when I visited his headquarters there two years later. For legal reasons, while in New Zealand he performed only spiritual operations.

People form in long queues to pass in front of him, and the spirit entity he is working with at the time gives them instructions on what to do next. For some it means an operation, while others are told to sit in with other people in adjacent rooms and meditate. This is referred to as 'sitting in current', which means that the energy being generated is its own form of healing. This is a very simplified explanation of the whole process: for full details and further explanations go to www.johnofgod.com.

Prior to standing in line to actually pass before John of God people write on a piece of paper what aspect of their lives requires healing, be it physical, mental, emotional or even spiritual. This message is conveyed in Portuguese to John of God, who does not speak English, by an interpreter, then the spirit entity decides what is needed at that time. Those selected for spiritual operations are later joined by João, who performs procedures them. Afterwards they return to their accommodation to rest and recuperate for the next 24 hours.

I still don't know to this day what inspired me to ask that I simply wished to *release the past*. However, my request was noted and the operation performed, and a couple of days later we returned to Australia.

A few days after we got home my skin started to erupt, and within a week about 80 per cent of my body was enflamed by red, raw eczema that covered me from head to toe. In great pain, I sought various forms of healing from energy healers and also my next-door neighbour, Ian White, who owns and creates Australian Bush Flower Essences (www.ausflowers.com.au).

Fortunately for me Ian is a highly skilled naturopath and was able to help me to control and then eliminate my eczema through diet and his wonderful essences. Ian and the other healers I consulted all agreed that by making such a sweeping request as 'letting go of my past' I was asking for trouble. It would seem that I got what I asked for, and my skin outbreak represented — as one of them told me with a laugh — clearing 'everything from my past lives, right back to the swamp'. It was one very dramatic way to balance my karma, and one that I would not recommend to anyone else.

Consulting my guide as I write this chapter, I am reliably informed that the message did come as spiritual advice. Although it was dramatic and very painful, apparently I was able to clear all my past karmic debt right up to that time, so with the benefit of hindsight I am grateful for the opportunity.

If anyone reading this is tempted to do the same thing, all I can say is be prepared for anything that may come your way afterwards. Who knows what secrets your past may contain? It's hard enough to remember everything we have done in this incarnation, let alone going back over possibly thousands of years.

Be careful what you ask for, because you may get it.

Chapter 19

PSYCHIC CORDS AND PAST LIVES

One of my favourite guests on *RadioOutThere* is Sydney psychic, palmist, teacher and well-known author Paul Fenton-Smith. Paul and I always have a lot of fun when doing a radio interview, and even more fun when we simply chat as good friends.

One of Paul's favourite topics is psychic cords, and in an interview on the program in October 2017 he unknowingly triggered in my mind an important link to past lives. Paul was talking about his book *A Secret Door to the Universe*, which has now been re-released in a new updated edition (Academy Publishing, 2017). The interview inevitably turned to psychic cords, which Paul explained to my audience as 'invisible cords of psychic energy that pass between friends, family and colleagues every day'. Each time we have an interaction with someone a psychic cord is established with that person. If it is a brief association the cord dissolves naturally after a few hours, but if it is an ongoing encounter more permanent energy cords can be established. The more cords that remain in place over a long period the more effect it will have on the person concerned.

This can lead to complications around emotions, physical health and our general well-being. The fact that so many people are still 'corded' to others who may be draining their energy or creating emotional conditions from anger to depression is one reason why there are so many troubled people in the community these days. The good news is that these invisible cords can be removed by bathing in salt water, taking a bath with at least one large cup of salt in it and also interestingly when we travel over the ocean, which is a very pleasant way to put the past behind us. Meditation and visualisation techniques also work. It is important to note that although *karmic* cords can be cut they will automatically reconnect until the karma is resolved.

Paul mentioned in the interview that once strong psychic cords are established we keep being unconsciously drawn to certain people over a long period. He added that there is often a karmic reason for this and cords can still be in place from previous lifetimes.

This hit me like a bolt out of the blue and, putting two and two together, I concluded this could well be the energy that inexplicably strongly connects us to someone we meet for the first time in the current lifetime. A karmic debt that needs to be recognised and resolved does not necessarily only play out with family and close friends. When we are strongly drawn to someone new in our life for no apparent reason, pre-existing cording may be the magnet that draws us together. It could explain things such as love at first sight and also experiencing reactions such as a strange familiarity with someone, an emotional or spiritual attraction and even a sense of discomfort or danger around the person concerned.

Those people we connect with at some stage in our life who are members of our extended soul family may be there in our life so we can both progress as soul energies. The interaction might be brief, such as with a work colleague, neighbour or acquaintance, but if a spiritual energy cord draws us together for a valuable experience it would explain a lot of the so-called coincidences in our lives.

It makes sense to me that if we are destined to connect karmically with another person in this life there would need to be some form of energy recognition at a subconscious level to which we can mutually respond. When I look back on my own relationship history, the concept of past-life karma being played out through past-life energy cords still in place explains many things. I have had four major partnerships in this lifetime, as well as several practice runs!

I first got married when I had just turned 22, and it surprised friends, family and even myself that I felt a deep need for commitment at such a young and naïve age. We had two children, one of whom my guides tell me is a member of my close soul family while the other is part of my extended soul family, which is sufficient reason for our relationship. I later discovered that my former wife Jan and I had a past life together long ago and there were certain unresolved karmic issues that brought us together; these played out over the 13 years of our marriage.

My second marriage was a case of love at first sight for me. I was part of a group undertaking a classic tour of Greece when I met Carol, the woman I would later wed. We had our first date in the village of Olympia, which is adjacent to the site of the original Olympic Games. As the anchor of a TV sports show at the time, the significance was not lost on me. It all went well, even though it turned out to be more of a group date than I had intended. We arranged to meet the next night in Delphi, the home of the famous oracle in Greek mythology.

I had teamed up on the tour with Chris, a young guy from Liverpool in England. In the restaurant we went to before I met Carol later that evening in a nightclub, Chris hit me with a question out of the blue. 'So, what's with you and this girl Carol?' To this day I am still shaking my head over the reply that sprang to my lips: 'I'm not sure, but I know that I'm going to marry her,' I said. He looked at me strangely and shook his head, obviously thinking: are all Australians as crazy as this guy?

The full account of how I went on to have an international romance with Carol, including the almost unbelievable way we met up again in Cairo, is contained in my book *No Goodbyes* (Tarcher/Penguin 2015). Suffice to say there is no doubt in my mind that it was no accident we were brought together as part of our destiny in this lifetime. That relationship lasted 12 years before we went our own ways.

The evidence for these past-life connections was provided many years later when I consulted a visiting expert from India who is an acknowledged adept in accessing the Akashic Records in the world of spirit. The Akashic Records, or 'The Book of Life', are alleged to hold the memory of all we have ever done, said or even thought. The title stems from the Sanskrit word akasha, meaning ether or sky.

Just using my birth date, the adept was able to describe my two former wives and our relationships in great detail. He told me there was past-life karma that needed to be resolved so I could become what he described as 'completely spiritual in this life'. He confirmed that all karma with both ex-wives had been resolved, for which I felt a great sense of relief. I can now accept that energy cords that survived into this lifetime could well be the catalyst that brought us together, so we could put the past behind us.

I have learned that my other two significant relationships, with my late partner Judy and current partner Anne, are also past-life soul connections and both started under unique circumstances. None of us was actively looking for a new relationship at the time we met, but everything just seemed to naturally fall into place. I have certainly had many karmic insights from being with both Anne and Judy, both of whom played a vital role in my three previous books *Afterlife, No Goodbyes* and *The Joy of Living*.

There are many people who find themselves intuitively drawn to a soul connection for a variety of reasons, and I firmly believe energy cords could well be one of the main catalysts. Perhaps a meaningful relationship will only blossom beyond a superficial initial attraction if there is some kind of karmic cord or agreed destiny path in place. Whether there is a direct past-life connection or not there could well be karmic lessons to be learned by one or both partners; these lessons would arise during the relationship.

Legendary reporter for the *The New Yorker*, Lilian Ross, summed it up well in her memoir *Here But Not Here* (Random House, 1998). The book described her 40-year relationship with the magazine's editor, William Shawn. 'We were drawn to each other from the first by all the elusive forces that people have been trying to pin down from the beginning of time.'

Chapter 20

MICHAEL NEWTON'S UNPUBLISHED REGRESSIONS

The late Dr Michael Newton is regarded as being a world leader in past-life work and life-between-lives research. His books *Journey of Souls, Destiny of Souls and Life Between Lives* are all international bestsellers. Michael Newton passed from this life in 2016, leaving behind a legacy that will live on for generations. A qualified counselling psychologist, master hypnotherapist and teacher, his academic qualifications were widely embraced by many higher educational institutions.

During the intense research he conducted, Michael Newton regressed thousands of people before actually writing his books. The Newton Institute website (https://bit.ly/2LzCZzy) states: 'Following discoveries in clinical practice, Michael began to explore the afterlife through the eyes of his clients. It was to be over 25 years before Michael first shared his work with the world, having researched and assembled a model of the spiritual realm through the eyes of 7000 souls and over a career spanning 35 years.'

Peter Smith, who wrote the introduction to *Past Lives Unveiled* and also regressed me to previous lives in Ancient Greece and the

US Civil War (described in chapters 3 and 11), is at the time of writing the international president of the Newton Institute. I was very honoured to be asked to do the radio tribute program to Michael Newton in 2016 on *RadioOutThere*, and have always felt a strong link to Dr Newton and his work. Peter has graciously given the institute's permission to include in this book some previously unpublished research by Michael; it was released in their magazine in 2017.

Marian's story

Two sisters living hundreds of miles apart in the United States were regressed by Dr Newton in separate sessions, and the information that emerged breaks old barriers of past-life research. Michael referred to these women (not their real names) as Marian, a teacher aged 29, and Deanna, a massage therapist aged 36. Marian was initially hypnotically regressed; no thought was given at the time to regressing her sister (see later in this chapter for Deanna's regression).

In her journey into the past Marian went back to her life as a man in a Stone Age tribe some 30,000 years ago, much to Michael's surprise. She described her conditions at the time as 'cold ... I'm dirty, very dirty, my matted hair ... everything is so filthy ... bugs all over me'. Marian lived in the cliffs in one of a number of caves connected in a line along a river.

In his research notes Michael referenced the limestone caves in Europe, which were 100 feet (30 metres) high and 1,000 feet (305 metres) long. If they were connected, the living quarters were extensive. Since Stone Age tribes needed fresh water close by, these caves were usually near rivers.

Marian responded easily to further questions, revealing that the name of this past-life incarnation was Ja and he wore the fur of a bear he'd hunted. Deer and cats were also hunted for their fur, as well as the food they provided. Ja described encountering large, elephant-like animals with reddish-brown hair, domed heads and long, upward-curving tusks. He said they were much bigger than elephants, had bad tempers and were very dangerous. Michael's notes say that subsequent questions indicated Ja was describing woolly mammoths, which largely became extinct around 10,000 years ago. He also determined by the nature of Ja's description of the climate and the tools used by the tribe the Ka-Wa, that Marian's past life dated back to somewhere between 30,000 and 35,000 years ago.

Ja went on to talk about the leader of their tribe, a very large, extremely violent man he referred to as Kahn: 'He is the strongest now ... BIG ... eats a lot ... but you can't trust him.' Ja says that Kahn helped himself to any of the women in the tribe he wanted, including Ja's mate Ka-La. However, Ja was determined to fight Kahn to the death if he tried to have his way with their young daughter.

As she was being regressed, Michael had established with Marian that she would be able to use her current mind if needed to answer his questions, and she would also be able to reach backward and forward in time. When he asked Marian whether anyone in the tribe was with her in her present life she exclaimed: 'Oh, oh! My sister Deanna ... she is also my sister in the tribe ... called Shalo.'

Michael then asked Ja what work Shalo did with the tribe. 'She sews the best, and teaches all the young girls.' Ja went on to say that Shalo had cooking skills with plants, and was 'a determined leader in her own way with our women'.

When asked about his mate Ka-La's work, Ja described her sewing talents and her ability with sharp stones to cut out clothes and make spear points for the men to tie on to sticks for hunting. Ka-La was also being trained by Zori, the tribe's healer, medicine man and shaman. Ja explained how Zori 'takes things off trees … digs up plants from far away and then grinds them in a bowl'. Zori's mother was called the Wise Woman, and according to Ja trained her son in the ways of the healer. Zori was given special status in the tribe and did not have to work or go hunting like the other men. Ja described him as being dirty and spending a lot of time by himself, although he did have skills such as cutting tools, making fire and drawing.

As a shaman it would seem that Zori spent a lot of his time in a state of meditation. 'He can sit for hours and think, while sitting not far away from the entrance to the Place of the Chipped Rocks,' Ja explained. He was very uncomfortable as he described this as a place of great power. It looked like 'an animal at the centre with a big open mouth … jaws, huge, big teeth'. When pressed for more details, Ja described the animal looked like a monster dog with a long snout.

(Michael Newton learned many years later that an archaeologist had discovered a Paleolithic cave in Belgium that was 31,500 years old that had the skeleton of a massive dog inside. His footnotes to this session also referred to the many ancient sites of standing stones, which he associated with the description of the Place of the Chipped Rocks.)

Ja explained that a very powerful spirit lived in the cave at the Place of the Chipped Rocks, and it was believed that this spirit could provide them with food and good weather but also punish the tribe by bringing hunger, sickness and wild storms, which made them afraid to approach the cave. It was up to Zori to negotiate with the spirit to bring the good times it could provide. Ja also mentioned that Zori painted on the walls of the cave to appeal to the spirit to help his tribe. When asked if anyone went into the mouth of the beast, Ja replied with horror that there was great magic there and if they entered they would die.

When Michael asked Ja what he thought Zori was doing when he was at the front of the Place of the Chipped Rocks, he replied: 'He sits with his eyes closed and chants. But he can also be quiet, like he is praying.' Michael asked if Zori could be meditating and, if so, why. Ja agreed, saying: 'Meditating is better. He does this to communicate with the Great Spirit, to bring the positive aspects of the Spirit back into our [home] caves when he returns. You know, to help us ... give us strength from a higher power.' Ja added that it was also why Zori created the cave paintings.

Curious about the way the Ka-Wa lived, Michael enquired if it was a strong tribe. 'Yes, very,' was the reply. 'We are a big tribe and the others are very cautious around us.' Ja explained that the next strongest tribe to theirs was called the Tree-Waas. There was no inter-marriage with this tribe, as it was forbidden by Kahn. Ja believed it was because Kahn was afraid of being overthrown and did not want to risk losing the power he had over his tribe.

Continuing his research into life in a Stone Age community, Michael asked about tribal beliefs concerning what happened when they died. Ja said he would be buried with his best spear and his favourite rock knife, and would be provided with water for his journey. When asked where he thought he would go, Ja replied: 'We will rise into the white river of stars stretched across the sky.'

Further questioning allowed Michael to confirm that this is what we refer to as the Milky Way. His case notes also stated that this belief system is held even in modern times by such indigenous peoples as the American Indians and the Australian Aborigines. He also noted that in the pristine skies of that time the Milky Way would appear like a river.

He then took Ja to the last day of his life to explain the circumstances of his death, with the command that as death was about to happen he would rise out of his body so he could be a detached observer to the events happening.

Ja said that the tribe needed food so he was hunting with his two sons well away from their caves. He saw the 'huge animal with the long tusks', which ran at Ja after his sons tried to spear it. 'One of my sons grabs the hair on the side of its body and tries to hang on and turn him away from me. I throw my spear hard at his chest. It is no use, we cannot stop him and I am trampled to death.'

Ja told Michael he thought his age was near 40 at this time, and describes what happened after he was trampled. 'My body is broken … it is all bloody … They carry me to a place near our caves for burial. Ka-La is beside herself. I seem to be drifting above my body in a state of … nothingness. I seem to be rising and feeling no more pain.'

Michael noted that this regression was before he developed the life-between-lives regression practice, so he ended the session at this point. Marian was clearly exhausted by now, as during the session she had visited other past lives before reaching the one in the Stone Age.

In his footnotes to Marian's regression, Michael wrote that he had an interest in large 'memorial stones' around the world and has visited sites in England, Ireland and France. He also wrote of a visit to Rarotonga Island, the largest of the Cook Islands in the South Pacific, and after hiking for half a day came to a natural cluster of rocks known as a 'Marae', or sacred place, venerated by the earliest Polynesians. In the centre was a tall rock spire nearly 91 metres high that is referred to today as the 'Needle'. It was used as a place for prayers and offerings to the gods, and for the investiture of chiefs.

The similarity to Ja's description of the 'Place of the Chipped Rocks' is another piece in the jigsaw puzzle of the ancient standing stones scattered around the world. With more past-life explorations such as Michael Newton had with Marian and Deanna we may eventually recover a lot more about the purpose and activities surrounding these fascinating stones.

Deanna's story

Several weeks after Michael Newton regressed Marian he regressed her sister, Deanna. His notes say: 'When we first met Deanna swore that Marian had revealed nothing to her about her regression and their relationship in the Stone Age tribe.' Michael decided to focus primarily on the cave paintings of Deanna's tribe and the social dynamics of her important role in the tribe.

Deanna described herself during the regression as being 'outside our caves ... looking at the mountains ... wearing some fur, but mostly light deer skins'. She said it was not very cold. She looked into the caves at her father tending a fire, describing him as being kind of thin and not as active as he once was. Her mother, she said, was warm and loving and holding her hand. Michael asked her name and that of the tribe. 'We are the Ka-Wa and I am Shalo.'

Michael then took Deanna forward in time to when she described herself as being about 15 and 'dancing at my coming out ceremony for womanhood'. Growing sombre, she added: 'It is fun for a while but I am worried because it has been decided by the tribal council that I should mate with Watam.'

When asked the reason for her concern, Shalo said tearfully: 'Because I want no man as a mate ... Kahn is behind this because the bastard gets a lot of support from Watam, who is being rewarded because he wants me. He is too old for me anyhow.'

Michael pretended he didn't know who Kahn was to see Deanna's reaction. 'The tribal chief, an awful man, a tyrant, but very strong. His size and strength is great. He leads well when hunting ... I have to give him that.'

Before proceeding further, Michael asked Deanna if she could identify anyone in her current life who was a member of the Ka-Wa tribe with her at this time Deanna appeared truly shocked by the revelation. 'Really! I don't believe this … it's my older brother Ja, who is Marian … Well, I'll be damned!'

Pretending he didn't know anything about Ja or the other people in Marian's life at the time, Michael asked Shalo for some details about her brother. 'Well, he lives in a cave next to ours, and I love Ja and depend on him to help me. I like his mate Ka-La a lot, too. Ja is a fine hunter, by the way.' When questioned, Shalo remembered the harsh tribal leader Kahn in much the same way as her sister had in the first regression. However, she didn't know much about the Place of the Chipped Rocks, which she knew as the Broken Rocks, because Kahn forbade the women to go there.

Michael took Deanna forward several years in time and asked whether she had any children. Shalo was thankful she was childless, as having children would have made her even more subservient to the men of the tribe. Apart from her father and her brother, Shalo said she had no feelings for any of the other men. Michael then asked her about having sex with her mate, Watam. 'Well, we do,' she answered, 'but not a lot because I don't like it, so I don't give him pleasure.' Watam is apparently upset with her because she never got pregnant.

Shalo revealed that the tribal leader Kahn raped her occasionally, just as he did with the other women of the tribe. 'He forces me to the ground on my stomach with his powerful arm pressing the back of my head so my face is in the dirt.' Shalo expressed her hatred of Kahn and revealed that she had even planned how to kill him without Ja suffering from her actions, as they both would have been killed by the members of the tribe if she was caught. She eventually decided against it. 'Kahn is a strong leader,' she reflected, 'and his death could hurt the tribe.'

Knowing that Kahn raped her so he could humiliate her and make her afraid, Shalo worked out a way to fight back. She discovered that if she bit down on a piece of rounded deer skin as she was being violated it helped her not to cry out. When she found that Kahn regarded her lack of response as diminishing his status, it had the desired effect. Shalo passed this the tip to a few of the younger girls, and it lessened the attacks by some of the other men.

Michael asked Shalo a sensitive question and wanted an honest answer: 'Are you perhaps a lesbian?' After a pause, Shalo admitted that she probably was, which was not easy in the Stone Age society. She admitted she had feelings for another woman, but was reluctant to talk about it. 'We can only be together once in a while in our special place, and must be very careful. There is a ban on such things ... Children are needed because so many die.'

At this point Michael made note of the fact that Deanna had previously revisited six earlier lives, two as a man and four as a woman. He saw no evidence of same-sex preferences in any of these lives, including her current life.

In the next part of Deanna's investigation of her past life as Shalo, Michael asked her about the status of women in the tribe. Her response started with a derisive laugh, after which Deanna informed him that the men of the tribe, especially the hunters, considered themselves privileged. They look on women as possessions because they were physically weaker and thought women were stupid, which

Shalo said was a big mistake. Michael asked her about the reaction from these women's mates.

'It wouldn't do them any good,' Shalo explained. Kahn, as the biggest and strongest man of the tribe, had surrounded himself with other strong hunters to watch his back. These men got preference over the women they wanted as their reward, as along with the best cuts of meat. Apparently this was regarded by other Stone Age tribes as normal behaviour, and Shalo accepted it as being a part of life. She assured Michael that not all the men behaved in this brutish fashion, and some were nice to the women. The role of the males was to protect the tribe from the outside world, which Shalo and the other women appreciated.

Shalo spoke about her daily role as part of the tribe, which included keeping things orderly for the men, storing and preparing the food, making cooking tools and creating wooden bowls. She acknowledged her leadership role with the other women, although she said some of the older women pay no attention to her advice. Although some women were resentful of her actions it didn't upset Shalo, who described them as being set in their ways. Shalo's main theme of leadership was: 'There is strength in unity. Being passive gets you nowhere.'

Asked whether she was being passive-aggressive, Shalo replied: 'I counter my rebelliousness with positive things too as far as the men are concerned. I am skilled at making bowls and stone flints for crafting eating utensils, and I spend a lot of time, because I don't have children, learning healing methods from our medicine man, Zori.' These talents, and the fact that she was also an excellent carver of small figures using bone and ivory, made her useful to the tribe. 'The tribe likes my work, and I am generous with my gifts.'

Shalo went on to talk about Zori and his talent with cave painting, that he had trained two other men who she described as being 'fairly good'. Although women were not allowed to complete the drawing of animals on the walls, Shalo was allowed to sit in during the creative process. She was also permitted to sketch out ideas, and described it as being an honour when some were accepted by Zori.

Michael asked her to describe the process of cave painting.

'After we coat a section with a whitish clay, I am capable of scratching outlines of animals by hand on the walls. When Zori approves they are painted, maybe with some slight modifications.' While she described her abilities as being good as she had delicate hands, Shalo said she didn't want to give the impression she was allowed to paint very many animals to completion, as this was a man's province. Shalo confirmed Michael's question that her description of scratching is what we call etching.

Another note from Michael revealed he was testing Deanna with this question, because only professionals knew about the etching process in cave art that created a silhouette of the figure to be drawn first. Michael's original notes say that this convinced him of her authenticity.

Michael asked Shalo what kind of animals were prevalent on the walls of the caves she worked in. 'Oh, without a doubt it is horses,' she replied. Apparently horses were easy to catch and provided good food and skins, and some of the men were able to ride them while hunting. Michael asked Shalo to stand in front of one of the horses painted on a cave wall, and describe exactly what colours she was seeing and the appearance of the horse. After contemplating for a few moments, she described the painting of the horse on the cave wall as running. 'Her mane is black, also her nose, hoofs and tail, but the body is reddish-yellow.' Shalo giggled before revealing that the horse was pregnant, adding that they wanted to find more horses.

Michael asked her for more details of the other animals on the walls and why they were there. Animal drawings might appear right after an important kill, to preserve the animal's spirit so that others of the same species would come along in the future. Painting is also regarded as a sign of respect for the animal. Shalo mentioned drawings of elephants with long tusks (woolly mammoths), which she said were the biggest and most scary of the animals, and also cats, deer and black bulls with great horns, which were also very dangerous to hunt. Michael noted that she was referring here to aurochs, wild cattle that have now been extinct for around 400 years but were featured in many cave paintings.

Shalo surprised Michael by telling him there was no special place for paintings and they were all over the walls. He asked about the colours they used. 'Mostly black, from charcoal we use on sticks, then scratch the animal on the walls. This is most common. They also used reds and yellows, by collecting certain flowers and grinding them up in bowls with the soil before adding water.' Michael reminded her that her brother Ja said that animal fats were also used, which she confirmed.

Michael's note at this point mentioned that along with the

pollen from flowers, iron ore soil sediments produced red colours while ochre, a mineral in clay, was used as a pigment that generated a brownish-yellow colour. He added that in her conscious state Deanna knew little about prehistoric cave paintings, and her past-life knowledge startled him at this point.

When prompted to provide further details of the spirits of the deceased animals, Shalo said the women felt that these spirits gave them sustenance in their home caves. She said that her brother Ja and some of the other men wanted to acquire the strength, cunning and courage of the animals that were drawn on the walls. Shalo believed that they were also able to better communicate with the animals under their care whose images were on the walls.

When Michael asked her why there were no good drawings of humans, only abstract stick figures, Shalo explained that they didn't want their spirits captured in the same way as the animals in the caves.

Michael's notes stated that this was another test for Deanna, who did well with her responses. He explained: 'There is controversy among archaeologists about the lack of anthropomorphic figures in caves and my client's answer is one strong theory. However, I doubt that in a fully conscious state she would have known about this fact because the concept is rather esoteric even among professional anthropologists.'

Shalo confirmed that her tribespeople believed the spirits of all things on Earth live on after death, and by this Michael accepted that she was speaking of inanimate things as well. As Michael brought the session to its conclusion, Shalo told him she died before the age of 30, and from the details of her death he concluded she died from pneumonia.

Michael explained in his footnotes to this regression that he spent a lot of time with Deanna focusing on cave paintings to further his information on ritualised religious belief systems. He mentioned he had the same motive with Marian when questioning her about the Place of the Chipped Rocks.

Capturing the spirits of the animals on the cave walls is known as 'sympathetic magic', according to Michael's notes. The activities at the sacred stones and the cave paintings met the emotional and spiritual needs of the tribe. The superstition about and belief in supernatural forces did not take away from a conception of a spiritual realm after death, according to his notes. He believed the two sisters were not atheists in their Stone Age lives, and had a spiritual practice of some sort even if it came under the heading of magic.

In a further set of notes about these fascinating regressions Michael explained that he was using a practice known in hypnotherapy as revivification. Normally this process is divided into two parts: first with the subject being merely an observer while maintaining their modern viewpoint, and in the second process the subject's mind reverting to a past life in body and mind so completely that they vividly relived the events that took place. Michael was able to give his subjects pre-induction instructions and put them into a deep trance so they could combine both aspects of revivification. They were able to see, hear, smell, feel and taste in their past-life regression and experience such emotions as joy and fear.

He concluded his notes with this summary: 'I believe that the readers of the Stone Age lives of the two sisters can see that both Marian and Deanna were emotionally connected to their shared prehistoric lives in the caves, and there was graphic revivification in their animated responses. However, it was Deanna as Shalo whose answers were slightly more articulate in terms of insight and extrapolation.'

After reading the full details of both regressions, I totally agree with Michael Newton's assessment of the two subjects. These regressions are a very useful indication of just how far back we can go in time to explore our past, and demonstrate how many previous incarnations we may have experienced.

Chapter 21

OLD SOULS; NEW SOULS; SOULS FROM OTHER WORLDS

A question that intrigues many people is: where do all the souls come from? This is emphasised in the 21st century with the world population in a headlong dash towards the eight billion mark, estimated to be reached around 2025. Even with people reincarnating much sooner in recent times, there would appear to be a significant shortfall in the turnaround numbers as our population skyrockets. Statistics show that the annual death rate is around 40 per cent at best of the birth rate.

In my book *No Goodbyes*, I described a process in which new souls are created from old, advanced soul energies after they have returned to the afterlife from their lifetime spent on Earth or other worlds. My late partner Judy was channelled through Val Hood, a very gifted medium, and her description of the way new souls emerge is fascinating.

Val was shown the image of a light bulb that had shattered into many fragments, with a significant part remaining intact at the core. This dense core represented a collection of old souls and the fragments obviously became the new souls. When the bulb in this vision shattered, glass fragments extended outwards in all directions. The fragments furthest from the core represented newly created souls, while those closer to the core have already experienced several incarnations.

It demonstrated to Val and I that the original core energy could be taken as God, or the Creative Source, and the fragments have just kept shattering over the ages when they reached what we may refer to as a 'critical mass'. Each fragment becomes its own spirit energy, before eventually fragmenting again. I realised that this is another reason why so many gifted children have been born in recent years; their inherent soul wisdom combined with multiple past-life experiences is providing the people we need all over the world in these chaotic times.

Judy went on to give another example, that of an onion comprising many layers around the inner core. Each layer can be peeled off for whatever the appropriate purpose. The core stays the same, growing new layers as they are required. This core represents our true self, as opposed to our higher self, and each layer peels off in its predetermined direction. This will include other incarnations and the ultimate creation of new souls. Judy's message was that it doesn't matter how much we fragment; our core essence is still always residing in the world of spirit. This core spirit represents our oversoul and is with us in some way during our lives here and on other worlds. Each soul group from the original core sets out to explore and undergo every possible experience through its various members.

As a soul ends its life cycle in any part of the universe, the last incarnation is usually the most complex of them all as every karmic debt must be cleared. It explains why some newly created souls can just apparently sail through life with hardly any dramas or complication; they have yet to accumulate karma and deal with life lessons left over from previous lifetimes. However, subsequent incarnations will become more and more complicated as their life experiences help each soul evolve in its own unique way. They are often like preschool children happily playing with no thought for the future. The knowledge and experience they gain in their first school year will be the basis of their ultimate education. They will also start friendships that may continue for many years, even lifetimes, as well as making mistakes essential in their overall learning path.

With regard to an earlier chapter about soul groups, Judy revealed through Val that she and I are part of a core soul that fragmented many lifetimes ago. It appears that several members of my family, including my now partner Anne, are all part of this core energy.

This very graphic description of soul creation defines for me the concept of soul families, close and extended, as well as soul mates, which had eluded me until this channelling session.

Other-world souls

Freshly minted souls are only a part of the ever-increasing numbers needed to cater to the incredible population explosion we are currently experiencing on our planet.

It doesn't take a great deal of common sense or even logic to accept we are not the only populated planet in this universe, let alone any other universes and dimensions that may be out there. In my view, to deny this is extremely arrogant. If Earth, its people and our way of life is all there is, then it would mean that all those billions of galaxies, stars and other worlds are just lights in the sky to amuse us when night falls. The premise adopted by many sceptics is that humans are the most advanced form of life in all creation; what a disturbing thought!

Originally pioneered by Michael Newton, many life-between-lives-regression sessions clearly indicate that life on other worlds not only exists, but affects us directly. When he was a guest on *RadioOutThere* in October 2017 Peter Smith spoke at length about this, mentioning that Michael Newton's original 7,000 regressions have now blown out to over 40,000 case files in the institute, and current findings reflect this vast number of sessions. Michael Newton's case files reveal that Earth is a very *heavy* place in terms of energy and emotions, which makes it a challenging planet on which to incarnate. The energy is dense and the emotions are heavy. In our interview, Peter said that incarnating on this planet is regarded in the world of spirit as being very challenging.

'It's quite fascinating when people are regressed to a life on another planet where the beings have less dense bodies. Also, they don't have intense emotions like fear, anger, distress or depression in other worlds.'

As to my question about whether these worlds are more advanced than ours or just a different reality, Peter said that some of them are more advanced in respect of humanised form, while some are realities where there is no physical body like ours. In his book *Quantum Consciousness: Journey Through Other Realms* (Llewellyn Publications, 2018), Peter tells the story of a woman who went to a world where she found herself in the physical form of a giant squid-like creature living in the ocean. 'She was somewhat telepathic,' according to Peter, 'and described herself as like an organic satellite dish. Her role was to transfer information from the species that lived in the ocean to those on the land.' The purpose of her race of beings was to connect consciousness of various types of organisms that inhabited that world.

Peter almost sounded bemused as he recalled that the woman originally came for her session with the burning question of whether or not she was ready to have a baby. 'She wanted to know what it takes to have a baby and to nurture that child as it grew up in a troubled world.' As Peter said, she received an answer she didn't expect: 'If she could convey messages from one race of organisms to others then that's a lot of responsibility. She came out believing and knowing more deeply that she had what it takes to raise a child.'

My question was: can this be regarded as a real past-life experience, or in this case did her subconscious mind create a vision to provide an answer to her question? Peter acknowledged the latter possibility, but said that: 'The one sense of authenticity was the emotional response the client has to the information they are experiencing during the regression. It comes in visual, sometimes kinaesthetic, means; sometimes they can actually feel and describe the body that they're in.' In the case of the life as a giant squid, Peter believes there was a level of detail that went beyond imagination. Peter has found that people being regressed can make equally strong connections to life on other worlds as with their past lives on Earth.

Peter explained to my listeners on *RadioOutThere* how he has been specially preparing regressions to other lives and off-world experiences for some time now. The first step is to take the person being regressed to something that is a known memory, which might be someone's 10-year-old birthday party or perhaps the loss of a grandparent when the child was fairly young. 'We then go back to that memory and they experience the feeling of that memory, so they know what a memory feels like.'

Peter next directs them to imagine something, perhaps being in a restaurant with a famous person. He asks the client to imagine what the celebrity is having for dinner, and if they were to select a wine what would it be, along with other similar acts of pure imagination. Peter asks the client to recall the feeling of that experience and to feel it in their body.

'So, what they've got then is the feeling of a real experience and the feeling of imagination. They've tuned into the visuals and the kinaesthetic and also the auditory aspects of both experiences. Then I get them to pull out the other world or past-life memory that they experienced earlier in the session.'

Peter takes his client back into the place or situation they experienced beforehand and asks them about their reactions. 'Does that feel like the experience you had as a 10 year old, or was it like the imagination of the restaurant?' In Peter's experience, they reply that it is the feeling experienced as a child 100 per cent of the time. It makes sense to me that if we were to create a visionary answer to an everyday question about childbirth from our subconscious, surely an earthly set of conditions would be far more relative than a life as a giant squid on some far flung world?

I asked Peter about his findings regarding lives on other worlds before clients incarnated on Earth. Peter has conducted over 800 life-between-life regressions; he told me they are long, deep soul regression sessions, and wanted to establish the fact to my radio audience that there is a lot more to them than they realise. There is always a question he puts to his clients when they are in 'their deep and beautiful state and well away from conscious interference'. At this point he asks them: 'Have you ever incarnated on another planet or in another dimension?'

Of that 800 or so clients who were asked that question, I was surprised to learn only two have ever answered no. When they reply yes, Peter offers them the opportunity to be shown an important experience relevant to their current life. Peter says: 'I've had incredible feedback and experiences about where people go when they are invited to traverse the entire lineage of their soul to find a particular life that may be interesting to them in this human environment.'

I asked if these were just interesting or were relevant. 'Both,' was Peter's answer. 'Often we're shown a lifetime where it has some sort of aspect playing out in this lifetime.' He gave the example of a client who he described as being 'incredibly stressed and at a very difficult time in her life'. In a quantum consciousness session he took her through the quantum realms, and when expanding her consciousness further Peter asked that she be shown an existence outside of human form. She went to a large water world and experienced a life inside the body of what seemed to be a giant jellyfish floating in the water. 'She was turquoise in colour. The ocean itself had more of a purple tinge rather than blue, and she was in a place of deep and profound serenity.' This feeling stayed with her, and as she was an artist she went home and created a large painting of herself in that form. The painting still hangs on her wall and she stops and looks at it whenever she feels the need.

My observation about this past-life story was: why would anyone want to come to our world after living such a beautiful and peaceful life? Peter's reply summed it up for everyone when he said, 'Obviously, the tougher the school, the quicker the development.' He added, 'To spend some time here adds to a rapid development of the soul, and we simply undertake a journey to rediscover our magnificence as we learn things along the way.'

When I thought about this scenario it occurred to me that it is very easy to float through life, but at the end of it what have you really achieved apart from a peaceful floating feeling? When we live a full life on a planet such as Earth with all its ups and downs, we have the opportunity for a multitude of experiences and significant soul development.

Peter's research shows that a lot of souls who have other world lineage are now incarnating as part of the transition of consciousness through which our planet is going. 'Just by incarnating here with the lineage of their soul they're changing human consciousness because they are sending a different frequency into the collective.'

This led me to ask Peter whether in his life-between-lives regressions he has found souls who have lives on other worlds in between their lives on Earth. His reply took us into much deeper waters: 'Because there is no such thing as linear time in the spirit world, something Michael Newton defined as *now time*, how long we are there doesn't matter. We have always found a great range of activities people are involved in in the spirit world.'

As I have revealed in my books on the afterlife, Peter confirmed that spirits often work with energy they learn from other spirits there, and then incorporate this into their next life. However, Peter's life-between-lives regressions have divulged that some people talk of visiting other worlds during their sojourn in between Earthly lives. This can be due to curiosity or a desire to observe how other people live on different worlds to ours. It seems obvious that visiting these worlds can certainly be an important part of the planning process for someone's future life on Earth. As part of a new generation of advanced souls that are incarnating in the 21st century, they are potentially able to bring new ideas and information with them to influence our rapidly changing world.

Chapter 22

PARALLEL LIVES AND OTHER DIMENSIONS

The principle of multi-dimensions of reality is becoming more and more accepted in today's scientific world. We know that Earth exists in the third dimension of reality and scientists now accept that the fourth dimension is time, which governs the properties of all known matter at any given point (https://phys.org). According to superstring theory, the fifth and sixth dimensions allow for the existence of other possible worlds we are unable to see from our third-dimensional aspect. These worlds have the potential of being inhabited by lifeforms other than our third-dimensional human body. The theory states there are ten dimensions in all, with the tenth being the point at which everything possible and imaginable is covered.

There is a lot of speculation about the possibility of many more dimensions as part of the multiverse, with anywhere up to 26 in existence. Certainly, the existence of an eleventh dimension has become more popular in recent times. An eleventh dimension is described by certain physicists as a being 'characteristic of space-time that has been proposed as a possible answer to questions that arise in superstring theory'.

Inter-dimensional travel has been embraced by science fiction writers for many years as the explanation for why UFOs seem to be able to instantly appear and disappear. The previously unexplained phenomenon of crop circles that have been created over a span of many years is also being attributed to beings from other dimensions. It is feasible that if other-world beings are now embracing life on Earth in increasing numbers, some of them are more than likely to have lived in another dimension.

It becomes more complicated when the question of parallel lives is investigated. Peter Smith has done a lot of research in this area in association with Quantum Consciousness, a subject we discussed on *RadioOutThere*. Peter stated that there are two types of parallel lives to be taken into consideration. 'In Quantum we're looking at past lives because we are moving outside of time and space, where we see them in terms of planet Earth. Though they are past they are still unfolding, so they're parallel lives. Somebody can either incarnate now in the 21st century, then when they go back they can choose a life in the 1600s if they want to.' He explained that while this doesn't make sense in linear time, in fourth-dimensional *now time* reality it makes perfect sense.

Like most people I find it difficult for my brain to embrace this concept, even though the explanation offered by Peter makes perfect sense. To help explain further, Peter referenced some of the earlier work Michael Newton did while undertaking research for *Life Between Lives*, during which he found that a soul might incarnate in more than one body at a time. Peter explained: 'As we only bring a certain amount of soul energy with us into each incarnation, we leave a portion of our energy in the world of spirit. This enables an LBL [life-between-lives] practitioner to contact and communicate with that energy. Certain souls choose to split their energy between two different bodies so that they can experience completely different lives running parallel in linear time and usually having no contact with each other.'

Peter told the story of a client whom he took into an LBL session, asking how much soul energy she had brought back with her this time. He was surprised when the woman replied 40 per cent, as this is very low. To double check he asked her to confirm that she had left 60 per cent in the spirit realm, to which she replied: 'Oh, no, twenty.' As a former banker, Peter joked that those numbers didn't make sense and asked: 'What about the other forty per cent?' Peter said that even though she was in trance she gave him one of those 'what a stupid question' looks before stating quite matter of factly: 'In China.' Peter asked what was it doing in China, and she replied, 'Working in an office.'

Peter was really intrigued by now and asked her: 'Will the two of you ever meet?' Again he was given that look, before the client replied: 'Well, what would be the point of that?' She explained that she split her soul energy into two bodies so she could cover more ground and learn more. She was than able to describe the man in China as a 'middle manager working in an office in Beijing'. It was a very different life from hers and her soul was able to learn new things: another language, a different culture and, of course, experience two different genders. The level of derision the woman had for Peter's questions confirmed for him the authenticity of the soul contact. As Peter said that based on Michael Newton's research this kind of energy splitting is quite rare, but it does create the thought that, if it is happening, who knows who and what a person's alter soul ego might be or what they are experiencing?

Soul splitting into different bodies is also very rare in Peter Smith's clinical experience, and in the hundreds of past life regressions he has conducted he has only come across three instances of this. The first was a case where the soul energy split and embraced the bodies of twins, because they wanted to understand duality. The twins were a boy and a girl living in ancient Egypt and the main interaction between them was a psychic connection, which Peter described as being very deep and profound because they shared the same soul.

He conducted another regression with a woman who had lost a baby in childbirth and was looking for answers. When she was taken into deep hypnosis the woman surprised Peter by revealing that the child was actually a part of her soul energy; this was a key reason for why she felt the loss of her baby so deeply. 'It was like she had lost a part of herself,' Peter said, 'which of course technically she had.'

When she received the insight, and she was then able to access the energy of the child that was a part of her, Peter's client was able to let go and allow herself to heal. The question that arose for me then was: what happens with conjoined twins? Peter was not able to provide a definitive answer but believes that this is more likely to be a joining of the bodies, not the souls. I later put this question to my master guide who is mentoring me for this book, and he confirmed that all conjoined twins have two souls.

Leading on from the question of soul splitting in earthly bodies, I asked Peter if it was possible to split your soul energy between a life on Earth and another world at the same time. Peter recalls doing an LBL session with Fiona (not her real name), whose soul was split between this life and another version of herself on another planet. Peter was able to ascertain that 40 per cent of Fiona's soul energy was attached to her earthly body and only 30 per cent in the other world.

'The reason for that,' Peter explained, 'was that the other world she was [living] on was far more advanced, was much lighter and didn't have the strong emotional feelings and tougher density that she had to deal with here. It was like Fiona had to put a little bit more energy into her body here than she did with the other one.' Peter was intrigued when he found that Fiona referred to herself by the same name in both lives. The person she is in the other world is telepathic, understands a lot more about consciousness and is more advanced than the earthly Fiona.

'We made arrangements for the two aspects of her consciousness to remain connected and to learn from each other.' The other-world Fiona was able to describe the planet on which she lived as well as the body she was attached to, which apparently resembled the body she had in her earthly incarnation. Peter believes from the answers Fiona provided that this other world is also a third-dimension planet in another part of the universe.

To add another layer to this complex area of research, Peter revealed that he has had several instances where the soul of the person being regressed has disclosed it is actually part of a collective unconsciousness. One soul energy he contacted communicated that the woman being regressed was actually the courageous part of that collective, which separated from the group consciousness and came to Earth to take on an incarnation as a person. 'She was approximately one-twelfth of the being, but it was enough for her to be incarnated in human form. Her role is to report back what was happening in human form, and the other eleven parts were absorbing the communication because they were also psychically and quantumly entangled. Everything this woman experienced in her earthly life was offered to the whole collective.'

Later, when Fiona listened to the recording of her session, she was as surprised as Peter was to find out the true nature and purpose of her existence. She had no idea what the subconscious part of her was doing as she was going about her apparently normal everyday life.

Peter recalled another case where a client came to him to find out why he had a tingling feeling in his head every night. Peter described him as being a very creative man who had done a lot of work involving indigenous healing as a shaman. He was absorbing information from his shamanic practices and from his other creative work, and it turned out that every night he was uploading it back to the collective. 'That information, particularly the shamanic information, was being shared with other worlds.' Another fascinating revelation that emerged during the session was that he was actually drawing this information directly out of Earth because, as Peter explained, 'Gaia herself is a sentient being, and she was holding a lot of this information herself.'

These stories were making my head spin. Peter concluded by saying: 'At times like this you sit there across from them and you just take notes.' The obvious question is: were these case studies all coming from advanced souls? Peter and his LBL colleagues around the world are finding that things are changing markedly because of the new direction in consciousness we are experiencing on Earth. No longer is the life-between-lives experience generally just a sojourn between lives for many of the people they have been working with in recent years.

'We're finding more and more people coming back here who are more advanced souls, and they don't have the need for the same amount of support in their network when they return to the afterlife.' Rather than going to their soul group immediately, as is most commonly found, these souls may just go straight to a classroom where they have been teaching between many lifetimes on Earth. As Peter put it, 'So they might just see their students first, or debrief with their guide, access the Akashic Records, or they may just know their own answers when they return there.'

With more and more advanced beings now incarnating on this world, the LBL regressions are reflecting that state of being. Peter believes that because of the changes taking place on Earth, there is in all probability what he terms 'a waiting list of advanced souls wanting to come here to be part of it'.

My imagination kicked in immediately, and I visualised this giant waiting room with queues of impatient spirits hassling the overworked immigration staff for a seat on the next Earthly Express. Bureaucracy in the spirit world too? What a disturbing thought!

As to the question of parallel lives being created in alternative realities as the result of a major life event, as in the film *Sliding Doors*, Peter said he has a major concern with this concept. While quantum science says this is possible, Peter raised the question of the soul being divided to create this parallel offshoot. If the soul has come to Earth for the purpose of experience and development, how would it be advantageous or even feasible to keep splitting the soul energy to create other lives in other realities for every tiny decision? Is there a threshold where the soul is happy to split into another reality in accordance with their intention to learn? Do these other lives even have a soul as we understand it, or are they merely holograms in a holographic dimension?

In this area of research, it would seem that quantum physics creates more questions than answers.

Chapter 23

TAHCHEE, AND THE INTRIGUING CASE OF FRANK TESCHEMACHER

Tom Smith first contacted me in 2001 in the very early days of my current radio program, which was on live radio at that time and initially called *Out There*. Tom had written a book called *The Tahchee Chronicles* (re-released as *Tahchee Returns: The Chronicle Rewrites*, New Beginnings Publishing, 2016), which told the channelled story of Tahchee, whose last life on Earth was as a rebellious and visionary Cherokee Indian tribal leader in the early 19th century.

Tom's previous life

Tahchee led a faction of the Cherokee tribe that had settled in the area west of the Mississippi River after the Revolutionary War, around 1783.

Tom connected with the spirit of Tahchee in the early 1990s after working with well-known North Carolina trance medium Gordon Hughes for two years. At first, being very sceptical about communicating with the spirit of a long-deceased Cherokee Indian, Tom was finally convinced and drawn in to the fascinating story of

Tahchee and his many, many past lives.

Tahchee's soul lineage dated back many thousands of years to the time of Atlantis and its legendary destruction, along with other global cataclysmic events of that era. His soul went from lifetime to lifetime in what can best be described as a chain of lives always linked to his people, who were evolving through the destruction and migration of several ancient civilisations and global upheavals. In one of the early trance sessions Gordon Hughes stated that 'it seems his energy from beginning to end is Tahchee'. Later, Tahchee revealed that his rebirth was an agreement to always come back as a Cherokee Indian.

Over the course of the next few years Tahchee recounted the amazing story of his people's long and complex journey over many, many years, starting as an agrarian outpost of the Atlantis empire and going right through to the current Cherokee tribes scattered on the east coast of America. When Tom asked why he was selected as the one to write the chronicles, Tahchee informed him that he too had a Cherokee heritage and the two of them had shared many lives.

In an interview I did with Tom in November 2017 on *RadioOutThere*, he described Tahchee as being 'a very reflective man who knew that he did some things wrong, but had to get this important message out about how his own people had to develop in a different kind of way in order to succeed'.

Tahchee first came through to Tom via Gordon Hughes in January 1997, and his opening words are captured at the beginning of *The Chronicles*: 'I am the Cherokee Tahchee, who watches over a high-minded kingdom, routinely enclosed by an unforgiving world. My people are keepers of a divine flame and endowed with the spirit of a wondrous creator. The story you are about to read is our untold history. Only with knowledge can there be understanding.

'Tahchee Wah has spoken.'

Tom agreed with me that it was highly unusual for someone to reincarnate as the same person in lifetime after lifetime. 'He always came back as a Cherokee, again and again and again. He was part of a group of people called Nunnehis and they were spiritual protectors of the Cherokee tribe.' Tahchee believed that the Cherokees were 'the greatest thing ever', and he kept reincarnating in this tribe to reinforce that ideology. Following the disappointment of a treaty with the white man in his final incarnation in the 19th century, Tahchee became a renegade for several years before returning to the fold. He even went on to work as an Indian scout for the army for a short period, such was his reversal of attitude.

Looking back on this last life, and still feeling his mission for his people was incomplete, Tahchee told Tom that he had to change his method of operation and had decided to contact Tom to tell the full story. Several months after connecting with Tahchee, Tom was able to confirm that he himself had what he terms 'some Cherokee DNA', as his great-grandmother proved to be of that blood line.

This saga appears to be a unique example of reincarnation, whereby a soul is driven to help his tribal brothers and sisters to evolve over many hundreds, perhaps thousands, of incarnations. After finding that he had shared certain lifetimes with the Cherokee leader over the ages, Tom was able to come to terms with what he believes is an important part of his destiny in this life.

When Tom asked Tahchee why he needed to tell his story in these current times, the Cherokee's reply was simple. 'I came to tell a story of truth. We have much knowledge that has been forgotten. The ancient ones speak of a time different from which you know today. Our people came from the south, a place of fire. We lived in a great nation that was not Cherokee, with large buildings and wondrous light …'

So began *The Tahchee Chronicles*, the story of a man whose soul has roamed Earth in many human forms over thousands of years to complete his ancient mission.

After rewriting his book with the guidance of the Cherokee Indian as *Tahchee Returns: The Chronicle Rewrites,* Tom felt the spirit of Tahchee leave his life, never to return. After tens of thousands of years, Tahchee's earthly mission is complete. The question lingers: will his spirit now find peace after such a unique trek through time?

Frank Teschemacher

Tom's story of reincarnation continued after he discovered a fascinating link to his last life in the early part of the 20th century.

Soon after our first interview about *The Tahchee Chronicles* in 2001, Tom was ready to let his publisher focus on selling the book and move on with his life. He needed a complete change of pace after spending several years digging into the dim, dark past, so he began travelling around the world to set up jazz programs.

In this life, Tom had been as a jazz musician playing a variety of instruments. He describes himself in the world rankings of musicians in the B Class, certainly not an A-lister. 'I've played with many famous people, but I'm always the one behind the curtains,' is the way he sums up his career. He has played with such well-known performers as Cher, Manhattan Transfer and Whitney Houston. 'I've also conducted a lot of these people, so if you went to one of their performances I was the one in silhouette behind the artist making the music happen that they were singing.'

Tom has always believed that this life is but one of many, but was amazed when he discovered the link to his previous life in the so-called 'jazz era' in the early part of last century. In an interview on *RadioOutThere*, Tom told me: 'His name was Frank Teschemacher, from Chicago. He played with a lot of famous people, [was] well known in his musical community, but he wasn't a household name.' Teschemacher performed with some of the top jazz names in the 1930s, such as legendary drummer Gene Krupa.

Tom first found out about his past life when Gordon Hughes, the famous North Carolina medium who connected him with the spirit of Tahchee, unexpectedly divulged in a separate channelling session that Tom had been a musician in his previous life. Without thinking, Tom blurted out: 'Wait a minute, I was Frank Teschemacher.'

Being a jazz historian, Tom was dumfounded when as he put it 'the words just fell from my lips', because he had studied the era of jazz musicians in the 1920s and 1930s. For some unknown reason Tom had always strongly resonated with the musicians of this era, much to the amusement of his wife, Lorraine. 'I even parted my hair like Bix Beiderbecke, who Frank performed with at this time.'

When he was 11 or 12 years of age in Years 6 and 7 his school mates were listening to the Beatles, while Tom was listening to 1920s Chicago jazz music.

Tom recalled the day his father, who was also a jazz musician, came home with an old vinyl LP that was part of the RCA Vintage series. It featured a well-known orchestra leader of the 1920s, Paul Whiteman, playing a song called 'Nobody's Sweetheart Now'. Tom said of the occasion: 'The moment I heard that tune the light went on, and from that time on all I wanted to do was to become a jazz musician.' As Tom later discovered, that song turned out to be one of the ones that Teschemacher not only recorded, but was well known for at the time.

'That's pretty creepy, let's be honest,' Tom mused in our interview. As a student of the genre of music Tom had to do a lot of digging for information, as well as buying a collection of old 78 rpm records. 'I used to go to bed with headphones on listening to Louis Armstrong music when he was a very young, serious jazz musician trying to make great strides in the world.' However, when he came to researching Teschemacher, Tom always wanted to skip over it: 'I didn't want to talk about it, I didn't want to study it, or be a part of it. I would move right past it, but I would study all the people around him.'

Looking back on this strange reaction, Tom said there was no reason for it and it made no sense at the time. 'As time went on I would look at this Teschemacher thing and it would make me feel uncomfortable. There was something about it that bothered me.'

There was also another musician, Bill Davison, known as 'Wild

Bill Davison', who went on to become a very famous trumpet player and performed all over the world, including Australia. In his early days 'Wild Bill' had a stigma that affected his life for many years. Tom takes up the story:

'He was driving a car in 1932 in Chicago in the middle of the night, and was involved in a traffic accident that killed Frank Teschemacher when a taxi slammed into his vehicle. The other musicians blamed him for Frank's death because they assumed he was drunk at the wheel, and he was literally run out of Chicago.' Wild Bill eventually showed up in New York some 20 years later and almost completely re-booted his career. 'He began to play with a lot of Teschemacher's older colleagues, who by that stage had forgiven him and let bygones be bygones, and as time went on he became very famous.'

Tom recounted that when Wild Bill Davison died in 1989, it seemed to trigger a period when Tom's life was turned completely inside out. It was while he was looking for answers to his problems that he met Tahchee and his life was changed forever. 'I'm now convinced that Wild Bill had something to do with it, because later on I got to know his wife, Anne Davison. She called me out of the blue, because someone had told her that I was doing research about Frank Teschemacher and she assumed I would [also] be doing research about Bill Davison.' At this point Tom had discovered his past life and was intrigued by the events surrounding that life.

Anne Davison was, in Tom's words, 'not into this clairvoyant thing', but she was having issues with a ghost who was causing her problems at the time. She was convinced it was Wild Bill's spirit who was visiting her, and asked for Tom's help to deal with it. After Anne's call, Tom marvelled at the synchronicity and was motivated to go on what he describes as a big search to find out details of the accident in which Teschemacher had been killed.

Tom was puzzled as to why the accident was such a big deal in Wild Bill's life. 'As time went on I used my research skills to reconstruct this entire premise that Bill Davison was not entirely responsible for the accident. Perhaps,' he reasoned, 'the taxi that hit the car was actually being controlled by a Chicago mobster who had had a verbal altercation with Teschemacher.'

Even at this stage, and despite the emerging evidence, Tom was uncomfortable about delving into Teschemacher's life as he still felt very uneasy about having anything to do with the musician. He discovered a picture of Teschemacher in a musical encyclopaedia and found it difficult to even look at it. However, the evidence for the link between the two men was mounting.

Tom's research into Frank's life revealed that he had been born with severely crossed eyes but grew out of it as he got older. Tom was surprised at this discovery, as he has also shared this condition in his current life. There were other similarities between them that played on Tom's mind. 'When he [Teschemacher] was a kid, puppies and dogs would follow him around mysteriously for no apparent reason. When I was a kid the same thing happened to me all the time.'

Tom rationalised that as a music researcher it made sense for him to find out as much as he could about the man if he had indeed been the musician in his previous life. He discovered that just prior to the accident Frank and Wild Bill had formed, in Tom's words, 'what would have been one of the first big swing bands of all time'. They had apparently been booked to perform in Guyon's Paradise Ballroom, a speakeasy run by Al Capone's brother 'Bottles', but Bottles started a fight with Frank earlier that night. Frank was a quiet, reserved sort of man, according to Tom, but he would 'blow up once or twice a year'.

Frank was a good, well-respected musician but had problems on stage as he had no microphone skills. In this lifetime, Tom found early in his career that it was imperative to work on his stage craft. 'I used to study mic skills. I got records of live performances from great musicians so I could hear how they were speaking over a microphone.' He remembers feeling that there was something inside him telling him to learn these skills.

His research into the past revealed that Wild Bill had become the front man even though he was not the musical director. Tom believes this upset Frank and a rift developed between the two. After the accident Wild Bill, who was not liked by many of his colleagues, was blamed for Frank's death, and his career went into decline for many years.

Tom has now accepted, albeit somewhat reluctantly, that he was indeed Frank Teschemacher in his former life and that he has returned as a musician in this lifetime to finish the work he was unable to complete previously. 'Frank was about twenty-six years old when he died, and he was just about to reinvent the universe.'

At the time jazz music was being played in a two-beat style, which was very popular in dance music such as for the Charleston. Frank

Teschemacher introduced the four-beat rhythm, according to Tom Smith, which turned into the jitterbug dance. The four-beat style was later identified with the famous clarinettist and band leader Benny Goodman, who became known as the King of Swing.

Tom found it intriguing that as a young man Benny Goodman used to follow Frank Teschemacher around, often remaining in hiding so he could listen to and then copy Frank's style as a clarinettist and alto sax player.

When I asked Tom if he saw any physical resemblance between him and Frank he said that he believed there was, and remembered looking and dressing similarly to Frank as a young man. They also share a strong Germanic family background.

Tom and Frank share expertise in the similar musical instruments they played. Frank was an acclaimed clarinettist and alto saxophone player and Tom wanted to play the saxophone as a boy, but his father, a professional trombone player, insisted that his son follow in his footsteps. Tom went on to play the trombone and has worked with many leading singers and musicians, although over the years Tom has often played the alto saxophone for his own enjoyment and is more than proficient with this instrument.

There is one further intriguing piece of evidence that links Tom with Frank Teschemacher. As part of his research as a Fulbright Professor of Music, Tom started gathering data about various musicians using spectrograph imagery. It enables a musician's unique vibration when they are playing to be recorded and then compared with other that of other musicians. It works on the same principle as fingerprints; everybody has their own unique graph.

Some musicians have obvious similarities, and on Tom's website (http://tomsmithjazz.wixsite.com/music, in the Storyville Archive section) the spectrograph images for Frank Teschemacher and Benny Goodman are close but easily distinguishable.

Tom told me that as he was investigating his past life as Frank he ran the spectrograph test for them both. He was staggered to find that the two graphs differed by only 0.05 per cent. Despite the fact they were playing different instruments the two graphs were almost identical. Tom described the spectrograph as 'a form of internalisation you can't initiate'. For those who demand some kind of scientific proof of past-life connection, this would surely make even a closed-minded sceptic sit up and take notice.

One further interesting piece to add to the puzzle is that when a taxi slammed into the Packard Wild Bill Davison was driving the top was down, and both men were thrown out of the car. Wild Bill survived, but Frank's head slammed into a tree and he was killed instantly. Tom Smith was born with a scar on his head, and as he discovered in his search it is in the exact same place as Frank's impact.

Taking into account the past links to Tahchee and Frank Teschemacher, it would seem that Tom Smith is releasing a lot of very different karma accumulated over many past lives. Over the years Tom has consulted many clairvoyants in his search for answers, and he says their reactions are all the same. 'Man, you have sure taken on a lot this time!'

In the light of all this, Tom has put out a plea to the universe that in his next life he just wants to take it easy. My own research into the area of continuing life shows that an advanced soul who may be drawing near to completing their earthly life cycle is often thrown a large load to bear as an opportunity to clear the past and move on in a completely new direction.

Chapter 24

MY OFF-WORLD INVESTIGATION

Peter Smith's research into lives on other worlds fascinated me and the stories stayed with me for several days. It came as no surprise when I awoke one morning shortly afterwards with the message firmly imprinted on my mind that I needed to research my own past to see if I too had experienced lives on other worlds as part of my soul's journey. Having had several past-life regressions in recent years, I was also curious to possibly experience the difference of life on another world or dimension as compared to my many earthly incarnations.

As usual, Peter was only too keen to give his support and take part in this investigation, the only problem being that Peter and I lived over 1,600 kilometres away from each other. I volunteered to fly to Peter's home town of Melbourne to do a session, but Peter felt that we could do an online connection and still achieve the same results on the basis that we had worked together previously face to face.

We connected via Zoom, a professional video program that meant we could see each other on a split screen. After a few minutes spent familiarising ourselves with this connection we were ready to go.

Peter took me into a special place deep in my subconscious and also requested my guides and spirit helpers to be part of the connection. This was a different technique to the life-between-lives and past-life regressions we had done in the past, and it opened me to any buried and more far-reaching memories that might be buried in my subconscious.

As Peter took me deeper and deeper I connected with the image of a very large bird as it soared high in the heavens. The bird had piercing dark brown eyes and a large hooked beak. Like no bird I had ever seen before, it had an ancient appearance with long feathers and reminded me of a pterodactyl in some ways, even though it was obviously a different species. When I merged with this bird's energy I looked down at the ground far below, and the words 'free as a bird' echoed in my thoughts.

I felt compelled to put into words what I was seeing and feeling at the time. 'I see a very barren world, no trees, lots of rocks, mountains squared off at the top … Dark earth colour and a greyish sort of sky, with clouds moving very swiftly in the heavens. [There is] a sense of being alone, of isolation.'

As I moved further into this scenario I saw a city on the edge of the barren landscape. It appeared to me to be a very unusual place, which for some reason I described as a 'technological world', with strange-looking towers and a greenish hue that surrounded everything. My initial reaction was: 'It seems deserted; I don't see any people.'

Peter asked me to allow myself to get a sense of the form from which I was surveying this city. 'I feel I am an observer. I'm not part of this world, just observing, as if I was still that bird, but standing in the wings taking notes.' At this point the word cataclysm came sharply into my mind, and then other words came tumbling out. 'There was a highly technical civilisation, then after the cataclysm the world turned barren. There is a cut off, a dichotomy where the city world ends and the barren world starts.' It seemed as if a large knife had sliced down at the edge of the city and from that moment a barrier was put into place. 'Outside it was a barren, cold, hard world.'

Peter asked if I was in my pure consciousness making these observations, or in some form of life. My immediate reply was that I was a visitor. 'It may sound strange, but I feel like I'm a time traveller, with the ability to move beyond time and space.' It soon became apparent my mission was to observe and then write a history so others could learn from my notes. Peter asked me to get a sense of my name and let it come to me very gradually, with perhaps a 'translation into human terms'.

As my mind slowly searched for the answer, I eventually replied that it was a short name. 'It sounds like Leeela or Leeda … It's Lida … L.i.d.a. Yes, that resonates.' Peter asked if that was the name of my people or my planet, and I replied: 'No, this is who I am. I am not a leader; we have no leaders where I come from. There is more evenness, we don't have leaders telling us what to do.'

(Note that in the following paragraphs 'he' and 'him' are used purely for reference, as gender was not discussed.)

Peter asked what my connection was to the civilisation I was visiting as Lida. I replied that I agreed to come here to observe and research on behalf of my colleagues. 'We are all researchers.' Lida then came up with some startling information about his own world. 'Where I come from we are on the brink of destroying our own civilisation through war, through pestilence. We are looking for answers, why are we making these mistakes?' When asked what he had learned from the world he was now visiting, Lida replied simply: 'There was no love.'

When asked to explain further, Lida said: 'There is just no feeling of love anywhere here. It was cold, technical ... There was greed ... many things destroying it, a complete lack of emotion.' When Peter asked at what cost, Lida simply replied: 'Total destruction, annihilation.'

When Peter asked Lida how he travelled to civilisations such as the one he was visiting, once again he received a surprising answer. 'You would call it teleporting. I am able to travel without physical form ...We are *all* able to travel without physical form.' Lida then went on to add: 'We do not have the same physical form as you; we are almost pure energy as you would understand it.'

When Peter asked Lida to tell him where his home world was, he replied: 'Far from here. You would understand it as another dimension.' Lida described his world as being 'not yet desolate, there is still hope. We do have colour, we do have emotion and we do have love, but these are being challenged. The world I am visiting has no colour, no love. Love went many, many aeons ago. The people who lived here became empty beings, they had no purpose beyond their own self-satisfaction.'

Peter asked Lida what else he had he learned from his travels about worlds such as this one. 'There are many, many worlds; some are inhabited and some inhabited in different ways. Life exists in many forms. We have been studying for many generations as you would understand it, in the worlds around us.'

When Peter asked Lida whether he or his colleagues had ever studied the planet Earth, he was puzzled by the question. '*Ert*; I don't understand *ert*.' Peter explained, and asked Lida to get a sense of the dimension he was visiting for this contact through Barry and to feel Barry's existence and all he knew about this planet.

'This is a much lower frequency,' Lida replied. 'Time as you refer to it has no meaning, no relevance, but as part of all there is what you call Earth is still evolving slowly. The frequency, or as you would say vibration, is much lower, much denser. I would find it, as would my people, very difficult to live in this atmosphere. I can visit, but I cannot stay long, I feel a restriction.'

Peter asked Lida to feel whatever was needed to get into a degree of comfort for himself while still remaining in contact with Barry. After a pause, Lida continued: 'I am able to sense his physical form, to speak with his mind and his thoughts.'

When asked whether he thought there was greater purpose in all that we do, Lida replied simply: 'Of course.' So what was the purpose of connecting with Barry in this energetic experience? 'I am sensing there is a connection; he is part of me and I am part of him. Strange,' he mused, 'a strange thing to feel. The more I feel here now, the more I realise I have a purpose on your planet. I have much to learn, I have much to tell my colleagues.'

Peter informed Lida that 'we have much to share with you, as our planet also has significant challenges that we wish to overcome'. He sensed that Lida and Barry's journey was somehow connected in that common purpose. Lida replied: 'There are no what you call coincidences. There is a greater understanding, a greater purpose before we move away [from our purpose] and forget who we are, why we are and where we are, and then we become lost. The more I feel here, the more I realise I have a purpose on your planet.'

Peter asked Lida for permission to use the information being shared in the book Barry was writing, and Lida wanted to know what the book was about. Peter told him that its purpose was investigating other lifetimes, other existences elsewhere in the universe; that the intention was to share stories that provides inspiration to our people, and return us to love and away from the absence of it. Lida said he was happy to be part of this. He continued: 'There are many levels of existence, many experiences, things every energy has to understand, no matter whether they are in your world, my world or on the other many, many, many worlds in existence. We have many layers we need to work through, and it is important [to realise] that each layer depends on the next and also the one before it. It is an accumulation of these layers of what you may call life, or lives. That is our purpose.'

When Peter asked Lida what he knew about these other layers relating to his world, Lida replied, 'I would know if I wished, but I have no need.'

At this point in listening to my recorded excursion into another dimension, it suddenly hit home that my voice had taken on a very different timbre. Immediately prior to this session with

Peter my voice was croaky, even hoarse at times, and I struggled with my breathing. During the recording my voice was noticeably deeper, quieter and smoother with no evidence of hoarseness, and it seemed to me it was not the voice I would normally associate with my everyday communication and radio broadcasting. It was as if I had indeed tuned into an outside energy that was speaking through me.

After a pause to gather his thoughts, Peter asked Lida what his purpose for living was. 'To help others,' came the immediate reply, 'to understand, to avoid mistakes that others have made on other worlds … To learn and grow, and not destroy. Many worlds are destroyed by war and lack of love. It is important we understand that love is the binding force … Understanding, tolerance, all these things are important.'

When asked if he could offer the people on Earth a message to prevent the cataclysm that he was researching on the world he was visiting, Lida replied: 'Understand, learn and accept the differences. There are many, many peoples in your world; they do not integrate; they are all separate. Until this separation can be changed there will always be problems. Everybody wants to be right; nobody wants to accept other people's beliefs, opinions, research. I also see in your world the technical reliance that was part of the world I am visiting now. When the world of the technical becomes the dominant force people lose touch with each other, they lose sensitivity, they lose love.'

Lida paused reflectively for a few moments before continuing: 'The word community comes to me. In my world we are able, hopefully, to keep our community despite some of the problems. Your world is having a problem with community. I am not here to tell you what to do. I am an observer; I record my observations and my colleagues will take this information and add it to what we already know about the many worlds that we experience.' Lida added that we might refer to him and his colleagues as record keepers.

At this point Lida started to struggle with what he called the dense atmosphere of Earth, as he was combining his own energy with that of Barry's. He described his own world as being lighter in frequency, colour and vibrance (*sic*).

Peter then suggested to Lida that he continue the contact with Barry. 'Lida, it would be wonderful for Barry to have you as a resource to make contact across time and space. Is there a way we can achieve that with the energetic imprint of the two of you?'

Lida thought long and hard before finally answering: 'I will be able to leave part of my energy with him, yes. To what purpose?' Peter replied: 'To help with the book, to help spread the message, because all the research you're undertaking of course has a purpose of learning. As Barry is a part of you he can help spread the information associated with your research. I'm sure he would want to work with you in this way and to extend the purpose that you pursue.'

Lida expressed his willingness to stay in contact in this way, but when Peter told him that Barry meditates regularly and changes his vibrations deliberately to access other places, he was puzzled. 'What do you understand by meditates?' he asked. Peter explained that

Barry moves into a space where he expands beyond the physical form. Lida said: 'That is a natural thing for us to do, we don't have to meditates [*sic*].'

Lida was silent for a few moments before exhaling loudly and saying: 'I am feeling uncomfortable in his body; some of his body is starting to reject me ... I am not comfortable.' Lida then agreed that he could move out of Barry's body and just use his voice, but asked again, 'To what purpose?' Peter replied: 'Your comfort, and to allow the connection with Barry to continue.'

With a long sigh of relief, Lida was able to release the energy contact with Barry's body. 'I am still connected,' he announced. 'I was beginning to feel as if I was losing part of me. A very strange, what you would say, sensation.'

Lida agreed that because of the very different vibrational rate of our two worlds, he and Barry could meet again when Barry left his body while sleeping. He explained further about the differences between our two worlds: 'We are free to come and go and move around without the need of ... sleep ... A strange word,' he mused softly to himself. He went on: 'As I understand it, it is like recharging batteries. I have observed this before in other worlds. It is interesting: we have no need, we are able to dissemble our energy to be able to fragment it, so that we can, as you would say, recharge by fragmenting ourselves. We can exist in many, many forms and in many places at the one time ... *Time*, another strange word for me,' he reflected.

When Peter asked Lida whether he was able to sense Barry's guides, he replied: 'Yes, his unseen helpers.' When asked if they were familiar to him Lida simply said: 'They are part of all that is.' He then confirmed that he too had unseen helpers: 'Everyone does; there are many, many helpers taking different forms.' He confirmed he had different helpers for diverse activities. 'I am able to access these helpers when needed, but they are with me.' When asked how many helpers he had, Lida replied: 'I have never counted them ... Is that important?'

Peter assured him that we were also researchers, and to understand more of him would help us understand more of all there is. Lida explained that his helpers also worked with his colleagues, that they were a team. These helpers worked in relevant fields with his colleagues in 'what you call specialisation ... *Another strange word!*' After thinking about this for a few moments he added: 'But I do have, what you would say is, *a few* who are with me as my personal helpers.'

Asked how they served him, Lida was quick to point out: 'They do not serve me; I serve them. We are a team, we work together; there is no serving.' He agreed that describing it as an energy of mutual support, was 'a good way of putting it'.

When Peter asked Lida what message he wanted to leave with Barry he paused for several moments, almost as if he was tuning into Barry's energy again, before saying: 'His work is important ... He needs balance in his life. He sometimes moves in too many different ways, too many directions, he needs stability, as you would put it. Life is more than work. Work is important to all of us, but love is paramount.'

Peter asked Lida if there was any information we could offer him in return, and his gentle reply said it all: 'I prefer to make my own observations. As I am linked to Barry I will be able to observe more of your world, as is necessary. Perhaps we will come here for more research. Now I have seen your planet it is very challenging; we can learn much from each other. I will take this back to my colleagues.'

***

It was a weird kind of feeling I experienced when I first listened to the recording of the Zoom session I had with Peter Smith. My initial reaction was to remember bits and pieces here and there, similarly to the way I reviewed my past-life regressions. However, the more I listened the more I learned about our vast universe and my place in it.

The concept of connecting my energy with a being from another dimension is extraordinary, but to accept this is actually another part of me is mind bending to say the least. All manner of questions leapt to my mind as I listened again to the session while writing an account of this astonishing encounter.

Was I in some kind of dream state that allowed my fertile imagination to run riot and make up the whole encounter? Was some mischievous spirit playing tricks, or did I have a genuine experience as part of my extended research for this book?

Consulting my master guide, who is with me as I write these words, I have been reassured that I was indeed linked with another part of me from a different dimension of reality. My head swirling with possibilities, my guide made the point that while I am not some special kind of advanced soul, some 5 to 10 per cent of our earthly population co-exists in some way with a being from another world. In my case it is part of my life purpose, so that I can write about this seemingly bizarre connection to help people understand the concept expressed by Lida as *being a part of all that is*. My guide also confirmed that Lida was in effect one of my past existences, and that we are not currently living in parallel realities.

Looking once again at Lida's message to me at the end of the last chapter, it gives me the feeling that I am reading an assessment of my character after some kind of deep analysis. If I am completely honest with myself, which is not always the easiest thing to do, I will take his words to heart as being genuine, much-needed advice to help me at this stage in my life. They are observations for me to meditate on and embrace.

Another interesting point that hit me as I listened to my post-session chat with Peter was how my voice changed dramatically after I was brought back into this reality. It resumed the croaky hoarseness that had been with me that morning when I first spoke with Peter before the session. The two voices were very different, almost as if I was channelling Lida.

When I asked Peter for his reaction to the session, he described it as 'remarkable'. He told me that the information fit with his previous research involving life-between-lives and past-life regressions and also his quantum consciousness work. This research via other case studies showed that as civilisations mature they study other civilisations, something I had not heard of before this. 'As they evolve they want to get into the greater wisdom of the universe, as I have often learned from other researchers in the chair.'

Peter referred to Dr Michael Newton's teaching tapes, which are not publicly available, as referring to the 'time masters': those beings who are outside time and space. This means that they are able to travel energetically and in essence go anywhere inside time and space for their research. Peter maintains this confirms Lida's method of travel as being what we understand as teleportation. He also believes that if this travel is done with the intention of pure research the person travelling may not even know where they actually are in the universe, which opens up a whole new line of thought.

Peter also found it noteworthy that Lida referred to a world that is lighter in density, but found it most interesting when he spoke about colour, which has its own vibrancy. This is also the case in the afterlife, according to my research, where the colours are more vibrant to those in our third-dimensional world. Peter supported this with some of his other research into other-dimensional realities.

Peter made the point that as he watched me during the session, he noted that when I connected with Lida it was immediately obvious in my physical reaction. His reaction was definite: 'It wasn't *Barry*, as in energetic presence. There was something else there, and it was quite different from how I experience your energy normally.'

This is quite common for Peter during his clinic sessions with clients doing past-life regression, and he has witnessed female clients take on very male-type characteristics. This process is known as transfiguration, and it is also found when spirits connect with people during trance or deep meditation. Peter mentioned that when his clients go into a life-between-lives state the lines will often melt away from their faces and they appear as they did at around 30 years of age.

In summary, Peter was most impressed with the higher wisdom Lida brought through, including his personal advice for me. He remarked on the simplicity of the wisdom presented and said it was something that often occurred in these states of altered consciousness. To paraphrase:

'... *This work is important, but you need balance and stability. Work is important, but life is more than work ... and love is paramount.'*

Lida's words keep ringing in my ears.

As a point of validation, as we were speaking my friendly black and white currawong flew in noisily for the first time in several weeks and sat next to the open door adjacent to my office. He called loudly and insistently until I acknowledged his presence, which allowed him to depart. Peter heard the loud call from the deck outside and was amazed. As I wrote earlier in this book, the Aboriginal symbol for the currawong is *ghost wisdom*.

Chapter 25

WRAPPING IT UP

The research I have done in writing *Past Lives Unveiled* confirms one very important point for me: living multiple lives over countless years provides us with the opportunity to have as many experiences as needed to understand ourselves and our place in the universe as a part of 'all that there is'. One single lifetime, no matter how complicated, happy, tragic, challenging or successful, could never possibly contain all the experiences our soul requires in its pursuit of knowledge and wisdom on the merry-go-round of life in this universe.

Ongoing life is a progression of our soul energy as a part of the universal source we refer to as God. It is and never could be just a series of random events and chance experiences. My own regressions have been included here as I have been researching the whole area of past lives and reincarnation for many decades. Rather than reporting mainly other people's stories, which could be dismissed as anecdotal by some, I wanted to be the explorer and not simply the recorder.

My regression into my immediate past life as a young British soldier killed in World War I in France is documented fully in my first book, *Afterlife: Uncovering the Secrets of Life After Death*. Brian was part of the slaughter in the Battle of the Somme in 1916, and those past-life memories were vivid and very disturbing. When I stood at his gravesite while visiting the battlefields in 2010, I experienced a flood of emotion that was overwhelming. It was a release that needed to happen so that I could move on with my life.

My research reveals that I have led many lives as a soldier and a warrior, which explained to me why I brought back deep and unresolved anger into this life — anger that still flares occasionally as I slowly and painstakingly learn how to completely release this intense emotion. It has played itself out over two marriages and several other relationships, which proves to me how deeply we can bury intense past-life emotions that need to be released.

Even my life as Kasos, the Greek academic in Chapter 3, was tinged with violence through his association with the Roman soldiers. The same applied to my life as Jack, the British officer killed in the US Civil War. I feel that I have at last broken the chain in this lifetime, but I was in the school army cadets so maybe that was my final fling. I recalled that when I left school I did enquire about training as a naval officer, but fortunately a medical condition prevented that from happening.

In 2013 I was diagnosed with cancer, and the aftermath of the resulting treatment has opened new doors to deal with this long-buried emotion. The full story is written in *The Joy of Living: Postponing the Afterlife*, which I co-wrote with my long-suffering partner Anne, who I know is in my life to help me learn about the true nature of love. I'm probably in her life so she can learn about patience and tolerance!

When ancient Greeks went to consult the oracle at Delphi they had to pass through two gates to the temple. Written over the gateway were the words: 'Know Thyself' and 'Nothing in excess'. The oracle, representing the God Apollo, wanted people to consider these words carefully before seeking advice. The messages are relevant to our lives today, so it would appear we still need to be reminded of the importance of knowing ourselves. As for the principle of nothing in excess, our materialist world still has a lot to learn.

The true benefit of exploring our past lives comes in the form of understanding who we are and why we are here. When we can accept that we are more than just a passing moth dancing in the eternal flame before disappearing when our brief appearance has ended, we can potentially explore the full magnificence of life and appreciate the opportunity that has been provided for us to play a role in it.

Heeding the words of Lida, an aspect of myself from a past life in another dimension, the importance of love in our lives is paramount, both for us as individuals and for the human race. Civilisations come and go all over the universe, but Lida's observations are very relevant to our world as we struggle through the early part of the 21st century. I would like to leave you with his words, which for me sum up who we are, why we are here and what we can learn:

When asked if he could offer the people on Earth a message to prevent the cataclysm that he was researching on the world he was visiting, Lida replied: 'Understanding, learning and accepting the differences. There are many, many peoples in your world; they do not integrate; they are all separate. Until this separation can be changed there will always be problems. Everybody wants to be right; nobody wants to accept other people's beliefs, opinions, research. I also see in your world the technical reliance that was part of the world I am visiting now. When the world of the technical becomes the dominant force people lose touch with each other, they lose sensitivity; they lose love.'

About the author

Barry Eaton has a wide background in all areas of the media and entertainment industries. He is a highly experienced radio and TV presenter, having spent many years with the Australian Broadcasting Corporation and various commercial radio and TV stations. He currently produces and hosts the internet radio program *RadioOutThere.com*, now in its 16th year and enjoying a worldwide audience.

Along with his wide corporate experience through running his own media consulting company, Barry has scripted and narrated many documentary films and corporate presentations and written numerous feature stories for magazines and newspapers on subjects from astrology to travel.

He lectured in radio journalism and production at the Faculty of Journalism at Macleay College in Sydney, appeared in a number of films, stage productions and TV shows as an actor and has narrated a series of wildlife documentaries and video presentations.

Barry is a qualified astrologer, psychic and medium who studied mediumship at the world-famous Arthur Findlay College in the United Kingdom. Also an accomplished MC and speaker, he has spoken about the afterlife at many conferences and was presented with the Hall of Fame Award by the Australian Psychics Association in 2012.

His books *Afterlife: Uncovering the Secrets of Life After Death* and *No Goodbyes: Insights from the Heaven World* are the first two parts of a trilogy that will be completed with the publication of *Past Lives Unveiled*. The first two books received wide international publicity, including appearances by Barry on *Coast to Coast* in North America. Another book, *The Joy of Living* co-written with his partner Anne Morjanoff, addresses his alternative approach to healing throat cancer.

Other books by Barry ...

The Joy of Living: Postponing the Afterlife
234 x 153mm, 224 pages, paperback, ISBN 978-1-925429-48-0

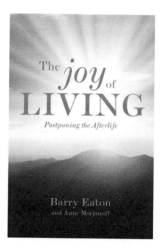

The Joy of Living is a story that touches the soul and gives us heart warming, fascinating and deep insights on the hard road from diagnosis to treatment and eventual survival from throat cancer.

Barry Eaton, author and radio presenter, describes the careful preparations he made for his journey, using his experience and understanding of the spirit world to deal with and survive the ordeal. Balancing holistic and spiritual methods with modern medicine, he found the means of coping as well as developing a deeper understanding of his life's purpose. Barry tells his story in his own inimitable style, sprinkled with amusing anecdotes and recollections.

Dealing with customary fears surrounding cancer, Barry's story unfolds with insights from his partner Anne and son Matt, as they support him through his emotional roller-coaster journey.

Available at all good book stores or online at rockpoolpublishing.co